God Bless You
Carol Schlegel

# Famous Idaho Potato Recipes

*Every Day....to Gourmet!*

## Volume 1

God's Blessings
Donna Lowrance

Printed by

CHJ Publishing
1103 West Main
Middleton, Idaho 83644

Printed in the United States of America

# Acknowledgements

We want to praise our Lord for the idea of this cookbook. He is the one who gave us the wisdom to put this together. He has caused people to cross our path to help us bring together all that had to be done to make this potato cookbook come into being.

We want to thank each and every one who have contributed to the making of our potato cookbook. We appreciate each and everyone.

We want to say thank you to Dan and Karen Smede for the cover of our book, it is fantastic. We want to thank Clinton Jones, of CHJ Publishing and Printing, for all the time he spent with us to put the finish touches on it.

God Bless each and every one!

# TABLE OF CONTENTS

# SIDE DISHES
# MAIN DISHES AND CASSEROLES

## MASHED POTATOES

6 medium potatoes
3 Tbs. butter
1 tsp. salt
1/8 tsp. pepper
1/2 to 1 cup milk or cream

Wash, peel and chunk potatoes. Put potatoes in a sauce pan, add enough water to barely cover potatoes, cover. Cook 25 to 30 minutes or until tender when pierced with a fork, drain. With electric mixer, whip potatoes until fluffy. Add butter, salt and pepper. Gradually add milk or cream. When boiling potatoes to mash, you may add to the water a small onion, a slit clove of garlic, a bay leaf, or a rib of celery. Remove before mashing. Serves 6.

## MICROWAVE MASHED POTATOES

4 medium potatoes
1 tsp. salt
3/4 cup milk
2 Tbs. butter

Peel potatoes and cut into 1 inch cubes. Place in a 2 quart casserole with 1/2 cup water, cover. Place in microwave and cook on high for 12 to 14 minutes. Stir potatoes after 6 minutes. Cover and continue cooking until done. Drain potatoes and whip with electric mixer. Add salt, milk, and butter. Whip until fluffy. Serves 4.

# MASHED POTATO CASSEROLE

4 cups mashed potatoes
1 cup cottage cheese
1 (3 oz.) pkg. softened cream cheese
3 egg yolks
1 to 2 Tbs. parsley flakes
2 Tbs. grated onion
3 egg whites, stiffly beaten
2 Tbs. margarine

Add cottage cheese, cream cheese, egg yolks, parsley flakes and grated onion to mashed potatoes, beat well. Fold in beaten egg whites, pour into a 2 quart casserole. Dot with margarine. Bake at 350° for 1 hour, or until lightly browned. Serves 6 to 8.

# MASHED POTATO CASSEROLE SUPREME

8 large cooked mashed potatoes
1 (8 oz.) pkg. cream cheese
1 cup sour cream
1 tsp. garlic salt
2 tsp. chives
1/2 cup melted butter
paprika

Combine potatoes, cream cheese, sour cream, garlic salt and chives. Whip until fluffy. Place in a greased casserole, top with butter and paprika. Bake at 350° until top is brown. Serves 8.

# SEASONED MASHED POTATO CASSEROLE

1 (3-oz.) pkg. softened cream cheese
2 1/2 to 3 cups mashed potatoes
3 Tbs. finely chopped onions
salt and pepper to taste

In a bowl, beat cream cheese. Add potatoes, onions, salt and pepper. Beat well. Turn into a greased 1 1/2 qt. shallow baking dish. Bake at 375° for 15 to 20 minutes or until heated through. Serves 4.

# COTTAGE CREAM POTATOES

2 cups cream style cottage cheese
3/4 cup sour cream
4 cups cooked mashed potatoes (no milk or butter)
2 Tbs. grated onion
2 tsp. salt
1/8 tsp. pepper
2 Tbs. melted butter
1 cup crushed cornflakes

Place cottage cheese in a blender to chop briefly and pour into a bowl. Add sour cream, potatoes, onions, salt and pepper. Pour into a buttered 2 quart casserole, brush with butter and sprinkle with crushed cornflakes. Bake at 350° for 45 minutes, then place under broiler to brown. Serves 6 to 8.

# ONION POTATOES

6 cups cubed raw potatoes
1/4 cup butter or margarine
1 pkg. onion soup mix
1 cup of water

In a skillet, lightly brown potatoes in butter. Add onion soup mix and water. Cover and simmer until potatoes are tender. Serves 6.

# CHEESE POTATO CASSEROLE

2 cups mashed potatoes
1 (8 oz.) pkg. softened cream cheese
2 Tbs. grated onion
2 1/2 Tbs. flour
2 eggs
1 tsp. salt
1/8 tsp. pepper
1 (3 1/2 oz.) can of French fried onions
1 cup grated Cheddar cheese
paprika

In a mixing bowl, beat first 7 ingredients together until smooth. Pour into a 2 quart casserole dish. Sprinkle French fried onions over potato mixture. Sprinkle with cheese and paprika. Bake uncovered at 350° for 35 to 40 minutes. Serves 4 to 6.

# POTATOES O'BRIEN

6 medium potatoes, peeled and cut into 1/2 inch cubes
1 tsp. salt
water
3 Tbs. oil
1/3 cup finely chopped onion
1/3 cup chopped green pepper
1/3 cup chopped red pepper
salt and pepper to taste
2 Tbs. butter

In a sauce pan, bring to boil potatoes and enough salted water to cover. Reduce heat, simmer 1 to 2 minutes, drain well. In a skillet heat oil, add potatoes. Cook, stirring 8 to 10 minutes or until potatoes are browned. Add onion, red and green pepper, salt and pepper, cook 3 minutes. Add butter, cook until heated through. Serves 6.

# FLUFFY POTATOES

4 cups mashed potatoes
1/2 cup light cream
2 Tbs. Parmesan cheese
1 Tbs. minced onion
1 tsp. salt
3 egg yolks
3 egg whites, stiffly beaten
3 Tbs. melted butter

Prepare mashed potatoes, add light cream, place in a sauce pan, heat over low heat until very hot. Add Parmesan cheese, onion, salt and egg yolks, beating well with electric mixer. Beat egg whites until stiff, fold into potato mixture. Pour mixture into a 1 1/2 quart casserole. With a spoon, trace a circle through top, 1 inch from edge and 1 inch deep. Bake at 375° for 30 minutes, or until mixture does not stick to knife. Drizzle with melted butter. Serves 6.

# FLAVORED TATERS

4 cups mashed potatoes
2 Tbs. butter
milk
2 envelopes cream of chicken cup-a-soup or cream of mushroom soup

Prepare potatoes, add butter and enough milk to make fluffy. Beat in cream of chicken flavor cup-a-soup or cream of mushroom soup. Serves 4.

# HERBED POTATOES

6 cups diced potatoes
1 medium diced onion
1 cup chopped celery and leaves
1/2 cup snipped parsley
1 tsp. poultry seasoning
2 tsp. salt
1/4 tsp. pepper
1/2 cup melted butter or margarine

In a sauce pan place potatoes, onion, celery and leaves, add enough water to cover potatoes. Bring to a boil and cook 5 minutes, drain. Add seasonings and mix with potatoes. Place in greased baking dish. Pour melted butter over top. Cover and bake at 375° for 35 minutes. Serves 6 to 8.

# RICED POTATOES

In a deep sauce pan, cook 8 medium potatoes with skins on, until done, drain. Run potatoes with skins through ricer, into a serving dish. Keep hot. Serve with gravy or cheese sauce. Serves 4 to 6.

# DILLY POTATOES

2 1/2 cups cubed potatoes
3 Tbs. chopped onion
1 tsp. salt
1 cup boiling water
1/2 cup cream
1 1/2 tsp. dried dill
dash of pepper

In a sauce pan, cover and cook potatoes, onion and salt in boiling water, about 15 minutes. Add cream, simmer 5 minutes, stirring occasionally. Sprinkle with dried dill and pepper. Serves 4.

# CREAMED POTATOES WITH PEAS

6 medium potatoes, peeled and quartered
2 Tbs. minced onion
1 tsp. salt
1 cup cream
2 cups milk
1/4 tsp. pepper
1/3 cup flour
2/3 cup milk
1 (12 oz.) pkg. frozen peas

Place potatoes and onion in a sauce pan. Add salt and about 1 inch of water, cover tightly. Cook until tender. Add cream, milk and pepper. Bring to a scald, not boiling. Blend flour and 2/3 cup of milk, slowly add to potatoes. Continue to cook on low heat until thickened. Add frozen peas, heat. Serves 6.

# PARSLEY POTATOES

6 medium potatoes, cut into 6 pieces each
2 tsp. lemon juice
1/2 cup melted butter
salt
parsley flakes

In a sauce pan, peel and chunk potatoes. Add 1 inch of water, cover tightly. Cook on medium heat until tender, but not mushy, drain. Pour potatoes into 1 1/2 quart casserole. Add lemon juice to butter. Pour evenly over potatoes. Sprinkle with salt and parsley flakes, cover. Bake at 375° about 20 minutes. Serves 4.

# FRIED POTATOES

Wash and peel 6 to 8 medium potatoes. Slice cross-wise into thin slices. In a heavy skillet heat 4 Tbs. of oil or bacon drippings. Add potatoes and sprinkle with salt and pepper. Cover and heat through. Remove cover, on medium heat, continue to cook potatoes until tender, turning as they brown. Serves 4 to 6.

## Variations

Chop 6 to 8 slices of bacon. Sauté until cooked but not browned. Add potatoes and continue as in basic recipe.

Sauté 3 Tbs. diced onion in 4 Tbs. oil or bacon drippings. Add potatoes and continue as in basic recipe.

Sauté thinly sliced 3 or 4 celery ribs. Add potatoes and continue as in basic recipe.

Sauté the 3 ingredients above together. Add potatoes and continue as in basic recipe.

# COTTAGE FRIES

Fry 6 to 8 cubed bacon slices in skillet. Drain all but 2 to 3 tablespoons of drippings. Add 6 cups raw diced potatoes to bacon and drippings. Fry until crispy brown. Turning frequently, season with salt & pepper. Slightly beaten eggs may be added to potatoes and cook until set. Serves 6.

# CAMPFIRE POTATOES

1/2 cup bacon drippings
8 medium potatoes, peeled and sliced
4 medium onions, peeled and sliced
2 tsp. salt
1/2 tsp pepper

In a heavy skillet heat bacon drippings, add potatoes and onions, stir. Cover and cook until tender, turning as they brown. Serves 6 to 8.

# FRENCH STICKS

2 Tbs. margarine
2 Tbs. flour
1 tsp. onion salt
1 cup of milk
1 cup shredded sharp Cheddar cheese
1 Tbs. chopped canned pimiento
1 (16 oz.) pkg. frozen French fries

In a sauce pan, heat margarine. Add flour and onion salt. Stir, add milk. Cook until thickened. Add 1/2 cup cheese and pimiento. Place French fries in 8 x 8 inch baking dish. Top with sauce. Sprinkle remaining cheese over top. Bake 350° for 30 minutes. Serves 4.

# PARMESAN POTATO BAKE

1 (16 oz.) pkg. hash brown potatoes
1 (10 3/4 oz.) can cream of potato soup
1 soup can of milk
1 Tbs. minced onion
3/4 tsp. salt
dash of pepper
1/2 cup grated Parmesan cheese
paprika
parsley flakes

Place hash browns in an 8 x 8 inch baking dish. Combine next 5 ingredients in a bowl. Pour over potatoes. Sprinkle cheese over the top. Garnish lightly with paprika and parsley flakes. Bake at 350° for 45 minutes or until lightly browned. Serves 4.

# CREAMY POTATO CASSEROLE

1 (32 oz.) pkg. hash browns
2 (10 3/4 oz.) cans cream of chicken soup
2 cups sour cream
1 cup shredded Cheddar cheese
1/3 cup chopped onion
1/4 cup melted butter
2 cups crushed cornflakes

In a large mixing bowl, combine first 5 ingredients and place into a 9 x 13 casserole dish. In a small bowl, mix melted butter with cornflakes and sprinkle over casserole. Bake uncovered at 350° for 45 minutes. Serves 8.

# DELUXE HASH BROWNS

1 (32 oz.) pkg. frozen hash browns
1 (10 3/4 oz.) can cream of potato soup
1 (10 3/4 oz.) can cream of celery soup
1 cup sour cream
2 Tbs. minced green pepper
3 Tbs. minced onion
salt and pepper to taste
snipped parsley
paprika

In a bowl mix first 7 ingredients together. Place in a buttered casserole and bake at 350° for 45 to 50 minutes. Garnish with snipped parsley and paprika. Serves 8.

# CREAMY HASH BROWN POTATO CASSEROLE

1 (32 oz.) pkg. frozen hash browns
1/3 cup minced onion
1 tsp. salt
1/8 tsp. pepper
1 1/2 cups sour cream
1 (10 3/4 oz.) can of cream of celery soup
1 (8 oz.) pkg. cream cheese
3 Tbs. pimientos
1 1/2 cups grated Cheddar cheese

Mix potatoes, onion, salt and pepper in a buttered baking dish. In a medium sauce pan, mix sour cream, soup, and cream cheese together, heat over low heat, stirring until well blended. Pour over potatoes, sprinkle with pimiento and Cheddar cheese. Bake at 350° for 35 to 40 minutes. Serves 8.

# MICROWAVE SCALLOPED POTATOES

1/4 cup butter
3 Tbs. flour
2 tsp. chopped chives
1 tsp. salt
1/2 tsp. dry mustard
1/8 tsp. pepper
1 3/4 cups milk
4 medium sliced potatoes

Microwave butter in a 2 quart casserole on high for 45 seconds or until melted. Stir in flour, chives, salt, dry mustard and pepper. Blend in milk. Microwave on high 5 to 7 minutes, or until thickened, stirring every other minute. Mix in potatoes and cover. Microwave on high 20 to 25 minutes, or until potatoes are tender, stirring 2 or 3 times. Serves 4 to 6.

## Variation

Scalloped potatoes au gratin: add 1 cup grated cheese to sauce and stir until melted.

# SCALLOPED POTATOES

4 cups sliced potatoes
1 1/2 tsp. salt
dash pepper
2 Tbs. flour
4 Tbs. chopped onion
1 Tbs. margarine
1 1/2 to 2 cups milk

Place 1/2 of the potatoes in a 1 1/2 quart casserole. Sprinkle with 3/4 tsp. salt, dash of pepper, and 1 Tbs. of flour. Sprinkle on half of onions. Repeat layers. Dot the top with margarine. Pour milk over top to barely cover potatoes. Bake 1 hour, covered, at 350°. Uncover and bake 1/2 hour longer. Serves 4.

# SCALLOPED POTATOES WITH MUSHROOMS

8 medium cooked potatoes, cubed
2 cups grated cheese
6 chopped green onions
1 tsp. salt
dash of pepper
1 (8 oz.)can of mushrooms, drain and reserve juice
1 cup sour cream
1 (10 3/4 oz.)can cream of mushroom soup
juice from mushrooms

In a bowl, mix potato, cheese, onion, salt, pepper and mushrooms. In a small bowl, combine sour cream, soup and juice. Mix with potatoes and pour into buttered casserole. Bake at 350° for 45 minutes. Serves 8.

# AU GRATIN POTATOES

8 medium potatoes, cooked with skins, peeled and sliced
1/2 cup minced onion
6 to 8 slices bacon, cooked crisp, drained and crumbled
4 Tbs. bacon drippings
4 Tbs. flour
2 cups milk
1 tsp. salt
dash of pepper
1 1/2 cups cubed Velveeta cheese
3/4 cup grated sharp Cheddar cheese
3/4 cup sour cream
paprika and parsley

In a 9x13 dish mix potatoes, onion, and crisp bacon pieces together. In a skillet, over medium heat, add flour to bacon drippings and stir. Add milk, stirring until thickened. Add Velveeta, salt and pepper. Cook until melted. Pour over potatoes. Fold in sharp cheese and sour cream. Sprinkle with paprika. Bake at 350° 45 to 50 minutes, uncovered. Garnish with parsley. Serves 8.

# AU GRATIN HASH BROWN POTATOES

1 (32 oz.) pkg. frozen hash browns, thawed
1/2 cup chopped onion
2 Tbs. finely chopped green pepper
2 Tbs. finely chopped red pepper
1 (10 3/4 oz.) can cream of chicken soup
1 pt. sour cream
1/2 cup softened butter
1 tsp. salt
1/4 tsp. pepper
1 1/2 cups grated cheese

In a large bowl, mix all ingredients together. Pour into a 9x13 baking dish. Bake at 350° for 1 hour. Serves 8.

# GRATED POTATO CASSEROLE

2 eggs
1 cup milk
2 Tbs. flour
1/2 tsp. salt
1 tsp. celery salt
4 medium grated raw potatoes
2 Tbs. melted butter
parsley

In a mixing bowl, beat eggs, add milk, flour, salt, celery salt and potatoes. Melt butter in a 1 1/2 quart casserole, spread evenly on all sides. Pour potato mixture into casserole. Bake at 375° for 50 minutes, or until tender and is set. Garnish with snipped parsley. Serves 4.

# SWISS POTATO CAKE

1/2 cup finely chopped green pepper
1 cup finely chopped onion
3 Tbs. margarine
1 (32 oz.) pkg. frozen hash brown potatoes, thawed
1/2 lb. grated Swiss cheese
1 tsp. salt
Dash pepper
2 eggs, beaten
1 cup milk

In a large skillet, sauté peppers and onions in margarine until tender. Add potatoes, cheese, salt and pepper to onions, mix well. Pour into a 9 x 13 x 2 inch baking pan. Beat together eggs and milk. Pour over potato mixture. Bake 350° for 30 minutes, or until golden brown. Allow to cool 5 minutes before cutting. Serves 6 to 8.

# HEARTY POTATO BAKE

6 cups hash brown potatoes, thawed
2 (10 3/4 oz.) cans cream of celery soup
1 cup sour cream
1 Tbs. minced onion
2 cups shredded sharp processed American cheese
paprika
parsley flakes

In a bowl combine hash brown potatoes, cream of celery soup, sour cream, and minced onion. Place 1/2 the mixture in 9 x 13 baking dish. Top with 1 cup shredded sharp processed American cheese. Cover with remainder of potato mixture and 1 cup shredded cheese. Sprinkle lightly with paprika and parsley. Bake at 350° for 35 to 40 minutes. Serves 8.

# POTATO TOMATO SCALLOP

1 medium chopped onion
2 Tbs. margarine
2 Tbs. flour
1/2 tsp. salt
1/2 tsp. oregano
1/8 tsp. pepper
1 cup water
1 cup canned tomatoes
2 tsp. chicken bouillon granules
5 cups thinly sliced raw potatoes

In a skillet, sauté onion in margarine until tender, but not brown. Blend in flour, salt, oregano and pepper. Add water, tomatoes, and chicken bouillon granules. Stir over medium heat until mixture thickens. In a 2 quart casserole, mix potatoes with tomato mixture. Cover and bake at 375° for 1 hour to 1 1/4 hours or until tender. Serves 6.

# CARAWAY CHEESY POTATOES

4 large peeled and thinly sliced potatoes
8 oz. shredded Mozzarella cheese
2 eggs, beaten
1 2/3 cups evaporated milk
1/2 cup water
1 tsp. salt
1/4 tsp. pepper
1 tsp. caraway seed
3 Tbs. melted butter

In a 2 quart casserole, place potatoes and cheese. In a mixing bowl, mix eggs, milk, water, salt, pepper, and caraway seed together and pour over potatoes and cheese. Drizzle butter over top. Bake covered at 350° for 1 hour, or until tender. Serves 6.

# TATER TOT SUPREME CASSEROLE

1 (32 oz.) pkg. tater tots, thawed
3 Tbs. minced onion
1 (10 3/4 oz.) can cream of celery soup
1 (10 3/4 oz.) can cream of mushroom soup
1 (10 3/4 oz.) can Cheddar cheese soup
1 cup sour cream
1 lb. crisp, cooked bacon, crumbled
1/4 cup finely chopped chives

Place tater tots in a greased baking pan. In a bowl mix together next 7 ingredients. Pour over potatoes and bake at 350° for 35 to 40 minutes, or until bubbly. Serves 8.

# POTATO MEATLOAF DINNER

1 1/2 cups cracker crumbs
1 1/2 lbs. ground beef
1 lb. ground sausage
1 tsp. salt
1 tsp. garlic powder
1/2 tsp. pepper
3 eggs
1/2 cup catsup
1/2 cup chopped onion
1/2 cup chopped green pepper
potato filling

In a bowl, mix first 10 ingredients together. Turn into a bundt pan that has been sprayed well with a non stick spray. Bake 350° for about 1 hour. Remove from oven. Let set for 5 minutes. Place platter upside down over top of meatloaf. Turn pan and platter over. Remove pan. Have mashed potato filling ready to fill center of meatloaf.

## Potato Filling

5 cups mashed potato
1 cup sour cream
1 tsp. salt
2 Tbs. butter
milk
1/2 cup grated cheese
paprika and snipped parsley leaves

In a mixing bowl, beat potato, sour cream, salt and butter. Add enough milk to make fluffy. Pile into center of meatloaf. Sprinkle with grated cheese or sprinkle with paprika and snipped parsley leaves. Serves 10.

# POTATO BEEF PATTY CASSEROLE

2 lbs. ground beef
2 tsp. salt
1/4 tsp. pepper
1 cup cold mashed potatoes
butter
1/2 cup milk
1 egg
2 large finely sliced onions
8 med. peeled and sliced potatoes
2 cups beef broth
salt and pepper to taste

In a mixing bowl, combine ground beef, salt, pepper, mashed potatoes, milk and egg, mixing until thoroughly blended. Shape into patties. In a skillet, melt butter and brown patties on both sides. Remove meat from the pan, brown onion slices in same pan. Layer the potato slices, onions and beef patties in a large, well buttered baking dish. Pour beef broth over top. Bake at 350° for 1 hour or until potatoes are tender. Salt and pepper to taste. Serves 6.

# POTATO MEAT PIE

1 lb. ground beef
1 (16 oz.) pkg. hash browns, thawed
1 1/2 cups sliced cooked carrots
1/4 cup tomato saucc
1/2 cup finely chopped onion
2 eggs
1 1/4 cups shredded natural Cheddar cheese
1 (8 oz.) can refrigerated crescent dinner rolls
1 tsp. salt
1/8 tsp. pepper

In a large bowl combine beef, hash browns, carrots, tomato sauce, onion, eggs, salt and pepper, mix well. Press meat mixture in an ungreased 9 inch pie pan. Unroll the dough and roll out into 9 1/2 inch crust, place over top of meat mixture, tucking about 1/2 inch of dough between meat and side of dish. Cut 2 or 3 cuts in top of crust to allow the steam to escape. Bake at 375° 20 to 25 minutes, or until golden brown.

## Sauce

1/4 cup tomato sauce
2 Tbs. butter
1 (8 oz.) can sliced mushrooms with juice
1/4 cup chopped green pepper
1/2 tsp. garlic powder
1/4 tsp. oregano

In small sauce pan combine tomato sauce, butter, mushrooms, green pepper, garlic and oregano. Simmer 5 minutes, serve with pie. Serves 4 to 6.

# SUNDAY MEATLOAF WITH POTATO FILLING

1 1/2 lbs. ground beef
1/2 cup chopped onion
1/3 cup chopped green pepper
1 cup dried bread crumbs
2 eggs
1/4 cup chili sauce
1 tsp. salt
2 tsp. Worcestershire sauce
1/2 tsp. dry mustard
1/8 tsp. pepper
potato filling
snipped parsley

In a bowl, combine first 10 ingredients. Turn half of mixture into a greased 9 x 5 loaf pan. Spread with potato filling. Top with remaining meat mixture. Bake at 350° for 1 hour. Let stand 10 minutes, turn out onto serving platter. Spread with additional chili sauce and sprinkle with snipped parsley.

## Potato filling

3/4 cup water
2 Tbs. butter
1/2 tsp. salt
1/3 cup milk
1 1/2 cups mashed potato flakes
1 egg, beaten
1/2 cup grated Cheddar cheese

In a sauce pan heat water, butter and salt to boiling, remove from heat. Add milk and mashed potato flakes, stir well. Let stand until flakes are soft and moist. Stir in egg and grated cheese. Serves 6.

# POTATO MEATLOAF

1 1/2 lbs. ground beef
1 1/2 cups grated raw potato
1/2 cup oatmeal
3 eggs
1/2 cup minced onion
1/2 tsp. sage
1/8 tsp. pepper
1 1/2 tsp. salt
1 tsp. garlic powder
1 Tbs. Worcestershire sauce
1 (10 3//4 oz.) can tomato soup
parsley

In a bowl, mix together ground beef, potatoes, oatmeal, eggs, onion, sage, pepper, salt, garlic powder, 1/2 Tbs. Worcestershire sauce, and 1/2 cup tomato soup. Shape into mound in a casserole dish. Add 1/2 Tbs. Worcestershire sauce to remaining tomato soup. Spread over top. Bake 1 hour at 350°. Garnish with parsley. Serves 6.

# BEEF AND POTATO CASSEROLE

1 1/2 lbs. ground beef
1 medium chopped onion
1/3 cup chopped green pepper
1 tsp. salt
1/8 tsp. pepper
1 (8 oz.) can tomato sauce
1 cup cottage cheese
1 (8 oz.) pkg. cream cheese
1/2 cup sour cream
1/3 cup chopped green onion
3 cups cooked diced potatoes

Combine ground beef, onion and green pepper in a skillet, brown. Add salt, pepper, and tomato sauce, simmer slowly. In a bowl combine cottage cheese, cream cheese, sour cream, and green onion, mix well. Place half of the potatoes in greased casserole, top with cheese mixture. Then add remaining potatoes. Pour meat mixture over top. Bake at 350° for 30 to 40 minutes. Servers 8.

# POT PIE DINNER

1 lb. ground beef
1 medium chopped onion
1 tsp. salt
1/8 tsp. pepper
1 Tbs. oil
3 medium diced potatoes
2 diced carrots
1 sliced rib of celery
2 (10 3/4 oz.)cans of golden mushroom
1 cup potato water
1 can of biscuits

Brown ground beef, onion, salt and pepper in oil. In a sauce pan place potatoes, carrots and celery in enough water to cover and cook until tender. Drain, reserving 1 cup of water. Add vegetables to ground beef mixture. Place mixture in casserole dish, pour soups, mixed with potato water, over meat. Top with canned biscuits. Bake at 400° until biscuits are golden brown. Serves 6.

# BEEF AND POTATO PIE

2 eggs, beaten
1 lb. ground beef
1 cup bread crumbs
1 envelope onion soup mix

Mix all ingredients together. Line bottom and sides of deep pie plate with mixture.

## Filling

3 cups cooked shredded potatoes, or shredded hash browns,
1/4 cup chopped green onion
3/4 tsp. salt
1 (10 3/4 oz.) can cream of chicken soup
1 egg
1 cup grated Cheddar cheese
parsley
paprika

In a bowl mix first 5 ingredients. Pour into shell. Bake at 350° for 45 minutes. Remove from oven. Sprinkle with cheese. Garnish with parsley and paprika. Return to oven for 5 minutes. May be topped with sour cream and sliced olives. Serves 6.

# CRUSTY HASH BROWN MEAT PIE

2-9 inch pie crust mix
1 lb. ground beef
1/2 cup milk
1 envelope dry onion soup mix
1 (12 oz.) can of mushrooms pieces, with juice
1/8 tsp. pepper
1 (12 oz.) pkg. hash brown potatoes, thawed
1 cup shredded Cheddar cheese

Prepare pie crust mix according to directions. Roll out for two 9 inch crusts. Line a 9 inch pie plate with first crust. Combine meat, milk, soup mix, mushrooms, and pepper, mix. Pour into pie plate and top with hash browns. Top with grated cheese. Place top crust over the pie and seal the edges. Slit pie crust with 2 or 3 small cuts to allow steam to escape. Bake 350° for 1 hour or until brown. Serves 4-6.

# POTATO TOMATO CASSEROLE

1 lb. ground beef
1 cup canned tomatoes
8 crackers, crumbled
salt and pepper to taste
4 cups thinly sliced potatoes
1 medium thinly sliced onion
1 (10 3/4 oz.) can of cream of mushroom soup
1 cup milk

In a skillet, brown ground beef. Add tomato, crackers, salt and pepper to meat mixture, mix well. Place evenly into 2 quart casserole. Place the potatoes and onions over meat mixture. Sprinkle with salt. Mix together soup and milk, pour over potatoes. Bake at 325° for 1 1/2 hours or until potatoes are tender. Serves 6.

# SUPREME SAUCE POTATO BAKE

6 medium peeled and cooked potatoes, sliced
1 lb. ground beef
3 Tbs. minced onion
1 (12 oz.) can drained mushrooms
1 1/4 tsp. salt
2 Tbs. butter
2 Tbs. flour
2 cups milk
1 cup sour cream

Slice potatoes into 1/4 inch slices. Place in a buttered casserole. In a skillet, brown ground beef and onions. Place meat on top of potatoes. Spread mushrooms on top of meat. Melt butter in skillet, add flour stirring until smooth, but do not brown. Add milk and sour cream. Cook and stir until thickened and bubbly. Pour over top of meat. Cover and bake at 350° for 25 minutes. Serves 6.

# 24 HOUR POTATO DISH

10 medium potatoes, cooked and grated
1 (10 3/4 oz.) can cream of chicken soup
1 cube butter
1 pint sour cream
1 small chopped onion
1 1/2 cups shredded Cheddar cheese

Place potatoes in a bowl. Put remaining ingredients in a glass bowl. Heat in microwave until melted, stirring often. Mix with grated potatoes. Pour into 9 x 13 dish.

### Topping

Mix 1 cup crushed cornflakes with 2 Tbs. melted butter. Sprinkle over top of casserole. Refrigerate overnight (at least 10 hours). Bake uncovered at 350° for 45 minutes to 1 hour. Serves 8.

# POTATO CABBAGE ROLLS

1/2 lb. ground beef
1/2 lb. bulk sausage
1 1/2 cups potatoes, cooked, cooled and shredded
2 eggs
1/3 cup finely chopped celery
1/2 cup chopped onion
1/2 tsp. garlic powder
1/2 tsp. pepper
1 1/2 tsp. salt
1 cup shredded sharp Cheddar cheese
8 to 10 large cabbage leaves
6 slices of bacon
1 1/2 cups water
1 cup tomato sauce

In a skillet, cook meat and drain. Mix together, first 10 ingredients. In a large kettle, steam cabbage leaves in simmering water just until limp. Drain well. Place about 1/2 cup mixture on thin end of each cabbage leaf. Fold in sides and roll to top. Fasten roll with toothpick. Place rolls in deep casserole. Cover with bacon strips. Mix water and tomato sauce, pour over rolls. Cover and bake at 350° for 1 1/2 hours. Makes 8 to 10 rolls.

# POTATO CABBAGE BAKE

1 (32 oz.) pkg. tater tots, thawed
1 lb. bulk sausage or ground beef
4 cups shredded cabbage
1/2 cup chopped onion
4 Tbs. margarine
2 (10 3/4 oz.) cans cream of celery soup
1 (10 3/4 oz.) can cream of mushroom soup
buttered bread crumbs

Place tater tots in bottom of large buttered baking pan. In a skillet brown meat: drain and pour over potatoes. In a skillet, sauté cabbage and onion in margarine over medium heat for 5 minutes, stirring often. Cover and cook on low heat for additional 5 to 7 minutes. Add soups to cabbage, pour over meat and potato mixture. Sprinkle with buttered bread crumbs. Bake at 350° 40 to 45 minutes. Serves 6 to 8.

## Buttered Bread Crumbs

1 cup fine bread crumbs tossed with 3 Tbs. of melted margarine.

# CHILI BALLS

1 lb. ground pork
1 lb. ground beef
1 egg, beaten
1/2 cup milk
1 cup of grated raw potatoes
1 1/2 tsp. salt
2 tsp. chili powder
2 Tbs. oil
2 1/2 cups cooked tomatoes
2 1/2 cups water
2 Tbs. chopped onion

In a bowl, mix meats with egg, milk, potatoes, salt and 1 tsp. of chili powder. Form into balls and brown in hot oil. In a large sauce pan, combine tomatoes, water, onion and remaining chili powder. Bring to a boil and drop meatballs into the liquid, cover and simmer slowly for 1 1/2 hours.

# SUPPER IN ONE CASSEROLE

6 cups mashed potatoes, divided
1 1/2 lbs. ground beef
2 (10 3/4 oz.) cans cream of celery
1 (4.5 oz.) can chopped olives
1/4 cup minced onion
1/2 tsp. salt
1 (15.4 oz.) can whole kernel corn
2 1/2 cups grated medium Cheddar cheese
parsley
paprika

Butter a 9x13 baking dish. Pat 3 cups mashed potato in bottom of dish. Cook ground beef, drain and add soup, chopped olives, onion and salt. Spread evenly over potatoes. Drain corn, and sprinkle over meat mixture. Sprinkle half of the cheese on corn. Spread 3 cups mashed potatoes over top. Add remaining cheese. Sprinkle with parsley and paprika. Bake 45 minutes at 350°. Serves 6 to 8.

# POTATO AND SPINACH LASAGNA

2 1/2 cups water
1 (5.25 oz.) pkg. au gratin potatoes
1 (10 oz.) pkg. frozen chopped spinach, thawed and drained
2 lbs. ground beef
1 medium minced onion
3 cups chopped tomatoes
1 (8 oz.) can pizza sauce
1 tsp. salt
2 tsp. Italian seasoning
1/8 tsp. garlic powder
1 cup creamed cottage cheese
4 cups shredded Mozzarella cheese
1/2 cup shredded Parmesan cheese

In a sauce pan, heat water to boiling, add potatoes and cook until water is absorbed. In a large skillet over medium heat, cook ground beef and onion, drain. Stir in cheese sauce from potato mix, tomatoes, pizza sauce, salt, Italian seasoning and garlic powder, simmer uncovered for 20 minutes. Spread half of meat mixture into a can buttered 13x9 baking dish. Top with half of potato slices, spread spinach over potatoes. Then top with half of remaining beef mixture, 1/2 cup cottage cheese, 2 cups Mozzarella cheese and 1/4 cup of Parmesan cheese. Repeat with remaining potato slices, meat mixture, cottage cheese and Mozzarella cheese. Sprinkle with remaining Parmesan cheese. Bake 350° for 45 minutes. Serves 8.

# STEW WITH POTATO DUMPLINGS

3 Tbs. flour
1 tsp. seasoned salt
1/2 tsp. pepper
2 lbs. beef stew meat
1/2 cup oil
3 cups water
2 (10 3/4 oz.) cans of golden mushroom soup
1 Tbs. beef bouillon granules or 3 bouillon cubes dissolved in water
4 medium carrots, peeled and sliced
2 diced onions
Potato dumplings

In a bowl, combine flour, salt, and pepper. Coat meat with flour mixture. In a Dutch oven, cook beef in oil until browned, drain. Stir in water, soup, bouillon, carrots and onion. Bring to boil, cover and simmer 1 1/2 hours or until meat is tender. Drop potato dumplings on stew, cover. Simmer 15 minutes. Sprinkle with dried parsley.

## Potato Dumplings

2 eggs, beaten
1 1/2 cups soft bread crumbs
2 Tbs. flour
2 Tbs. finely minced onion
1 tsp. salt
dash of pepper
4 cups finely shredded raw potatoes

In a bowl, mix together eggs, bread crumbs, flour, minced onion, salt and pepper. Stir in potatoes. With floured hands form potato mixture into 2 inch balls. Lightly flour each ball before dropping into stew. Serves 6 to 8.

# MASHED POTATOES WITH STROGANOFF

4 Tbs. butter
1 medium minced onion
1/2 lb. sliced fresh mushrooms
6 Tbs. flour
1 tsp. salt
1/4 tsp. pepper
2 1/2 cups beef broth
1 1/2 cups sour cream
2 cups cooked roast beef, cut into thin strips
Mashed potatoes to serve 6

Heat butter in a skillet, add onion and mushrooms, cook over low heat. Stir in flour, salt and pepper, stir, cooking until bubbly. Add broth, stirring until thickened. Add sour cream and beef. Reheat over slow heat, do not boil. Serve over mashed potatoes. Browned ground beef may be substituted in place of roast beef. Serves 6.

# POT ROAST AND POTATO DINNER

3 lbs. beef chuck or rump roast
8 medium quartered potatoes
8 medium carrots, cut into 1 inch pieces
4 medium onions, halved
1/2 lb. mushrooms
2 envelopes garlic beef soup mix
2 cups of water

Place the beef in a Dutch oven or roasting pan, cover and cook at 350° for 2 hours. Remove from oven and arrange vegetables around beef. Pour the soup mix, blended with water, over the roast, cover and continue to bake at 350° for 1 1/2 hours or until meat is tender. Serves 6 to 8.

# MEAT PIE WITH POTATO CRUST

1 cup sliced carrots
1/2 cup sliced celery
1/2 cup chopped onion
1 (12 oz.) pkg. frozen peas
1/4 cup chopped green pepper
2 cups diced cooked roast
3 Tbs. flour
3 Tbs. butter
1 cup milk
1 cup beef stock
1 tsp. salt
1/8 tsp. pepper

In a sauce pan, cook first 3 vegetables until crisp but tender. Drain, add peas, pour into 3 1/2 quart casserole with meat. Brown flour in butter, add milk and stock from roast beef, salt and pepper. Cook until thickened. Mix with vegetable-meat mixture.

## Crust

3 cups mashed potatoes, seasoned
1/3 cup flour
2 eggs
2 Tbs. melted butter
1 Tbs. finely chopped parsley
1 egg white beaten with 1 Tbs. water

In a mixing bowl, beat together mashed potatoes, eggs, parsley, flour, and butter. Cover vegetable-meat mixture with potato mixture. Brush egg wash over crust. Bake uncovered at 425° for 30 minutes or until lightly browned. Serves 6.

# BEEF BIRDS WITH POTATO STUFFING

3 lbs. beef round steak, 1/2 inch thick
garlic powder
salt and pepper
melted butter
potato stuffing

Pound steak until 1/4 inch thick. Cut into 8 servings. Sprinkle with garlic powder, salt and pepper. On each steak put about 1/3 to 1/2 cup of stuffing mix, roll up. In buttered baking dish place the beef birds. Spread remaining stuffing between birds, brush with melted butter. Bake at 350° for 1 hour or until done.

## Potato stuffing

2 cups hot mashed potatoes
2 eggs, beaten
1 cup chopped celery
1 1/2 cup minced onion
1 (8 oz.) can chopped mushrooms, drained
1 Tbs. snipped parsley
2 Tbs. butter
4 cups cubed dry bread
water
1 tsp. salt
1/8 tsp. pepper
2 tsp. poultry seasoning

In a bowl, mix together the potatoes and eggs. In a skillet, sauté celery, onion, mushrooms and parsley in butter until tender. Soak bread in cold water and squeeze dry. Fluff bread and mix gently with potato mixture. Blend in remaining ingredients and mix well. Serves 8.

# POTATO MEATBALLS WITH SAUERKRAUT

8 strips of bacon cut into 1 inch pieces
1 medium chopped onion
1 (32 oz.) jar sauerkraut, drained
1 cup water
1 lb. ground beef
1 medium peeled and grated cooked potato
2 eggs
1/2 tsp. salt
1/4 tsp. pepper
1/2 cup sour cream
3 Tbs. chopped parsley

Brown bacon in a large sauce pan, drain, add onions and cook 2 to 3 minutes. Stir in sauerkraut and water. Bring to a boil. Reduce heat and simmer for 10 to 15 minutes. In a bowl, mix beef, potato, eggs, salt and pepper together. Shape into meatballs. Place over sauerkraut. Cover and cook 20 minutes. Spoon out meatballs and keep warm. Add sour cream and 2 Tbs. parsley to sauerkraut, mix well. Spoon into serving bowl and top with meatballs. Garnish with remaining parsley. Serves 6.

# MEAT AND POTATO PACK

4 hamburger patties
4 quartered potatoes
4 thinly sliced carrots
1 large sliced onion
1 large green pepper, cut into rings
16 sliced mushrooms
4 Tbs. butter
seasoned salt
1 (5 oz.) jar bacon cheese spread

In four large pieces of foil, place hamburger patties and vegetables. Top each with butter and sprinkle with seasoned salt. Pull foil together, fold at top. Bake at 350° for 1 1/2 hours. Remove from oven, top with cheese and serve. Serves 4.

# POTATO BEEF MUSHROOM CASSEROLE

1/2 lb. sliced mushrooms
1 medium chopped onion
3 Tbs. butter
1 cup bread crumbs
1 1/2 cups milk
2 lbs. lean hamburger
1/4 tsp. marjoram
1 tsp. salt
1 1/2 cups mashed potatoes
2 eggs, beaten
3/4 tsp. salt

In a skillet, brown mushrooms and onions in butter, cool. Soak bread crumbs in milk. Combine bread crumbs, mushroom mixture, meat and marjoram, mix well. Place in a buttered 2 quart baking dish. Mix potatoes, eggs and salt and spread on top of meat mixture. Cover and bake at 350° for 1 hour and 15 minutes. Serves 8.

# HAMBURGER PIE

1 lb. hamburger
1 medium chopped onion
1 (10 3/4 oz.) can cream of mushroom soup
1 (10 3/4 oz.) can cream of celery soup
1 cup sour cream
6 medium cooked potatoes, cubed
1 1/2 cups shredded Cheddar cheese
1 1/2 cups crushed potato chips

In a skillet, brown hamburger and onion, add soups. Mix sour cream and potatoes together, pour into buttered casserole. Add hamburger mixture over top of potatoes. Sprinkle cheese over top of hamburger, sprinkle with crushed potato chips. Bake 25 to 30 minutes at 350°. Serves 6.

# POTATO MEATBALLS AND GRAVY

1 chopped onion
2 bay leaves
1 1/2 quarts water
2 slices of bread, soaked in 2/3 cup water
2 medium cooked, grated potatoes
1 1/2 lbs. ground beef
3 eggs, beaten
1 tsp. salt
1/4 tsp. pepper

In a sauce pan, boil onion and bay leaf in water. Combine remaining ingredients and form into balls, 2 inches in diameter. Cook meatballs in boiling water for 10 minutes. Drain meatballs and reserve 1 cup of the water. Cover and keep cooked meatballs in warm oven.

## Gravy

4 Tbs. margarine
4 Tbs. flour
1 cup of meatball water
1 cup buttermilk
1 cup sour cream
2 eggs, beaten
1 tsp. salt
dash of pepper

In a skillet, melt margarine, blend in flour. Slowly add water, buttermilk and sour cream, heat until bubbly. Remove from stove. Stir in eggs, salt and pepper. Pour over meatballs. Serves 6.

# POTATO TOP CASSEROLE

1 lb. ground beef
1 medium chopped onion
3/4 tsp. salt
dash of pepper
1 (15.4 oz.) can green beans, drained
1 (10 3/4 oz.) can tomato soup
potato topper-see recipe below

In a skillet brown meat and onions, stirring occasionally, drain. Add salt, pepper. beans and soup. Pour mixture into casserole. Top with potato topper in mounds.

## Potato Topper

4 to 6 servings instant mashed potatoes
milk
1 egg
2 Tbs. margaine
salt to taste
1 cup shredded Cheddar cheese

Add enough milk to make potatoes stiff. Add egg, margarine and salt to taste. Slowly add additional milk to make potatoes hold shape. Place over meat mixture in mounds. Sprinkle with shredded Cheddar cheese. Bake at 350° for 30 minutes or until well heated. Serves 4 to 6.

# POTATO MEATBALLS

1 lb. ground beef
1/2 tsp. pepper
1 large cooked grated potato
1 egg
1 small grated onion
1 tsp. salt
shortening or oil
2 (10 3/4 oz.) cans tomato soup

In a bowl, mix first 6 ingredients together. Form into meatballs, in a skillet, brown in hot oil. Remove from oil and place in 1 1/2 quart casserole. Pour soup over meatballs, cover. Bake at 325° for 1 hour.

# CHILI TATER TOT CASSEROLE

1 (32 oz.) pkg. frozen tater tots, thawed
1 1/2 lbs. ground beef
1 medium chopped onion
1/2 cup chopped green pepper
1/2 tsp. salt
1 clove of garlic, crushed
1 pkg. chili mix
2 (10 3/4 oz.) cans tomato soup
1 soup can of water
2 1/2 cups grated Cheddar cheese

Place tater tots in a large greased baking dish. In a skillet brown ground beef, onion, green pepper salt and garlic. Add chili mix, tomato soup, water, salt, and 1 1/2 cups cheese, cook over heat for about 5 minutes. Pour over tater tots. Bake at 350° for 30 to 35 minutes. Remove from oven, sprinkle 1 cup of cheese over casserole, bake 8 minutes longer. Serves 8.

# ONION AND TATER TOT CASSEROLE

2 lbs. ground beef
1 medium chopped onion
1 (10 3/4 oz.) can cream of celery soup
1 (10 3/4 oz.) can cream of chicken soup
1 (32 oz.) pkg. tater tots, thawed
1 (10 3/4 oz.) can Cheddar cheese soup
2 (2.8 oz.) cans onion rings

In a skillet, brown ground beef and onions, drain. Mix celery and chicken soup, add to the meat. Line bottom of a large baking dish with tater tots. Pour the meat mixture over tater tots. Spoon Cheddar cheese soup over top of mixture. Place the onion rings over top of cheese soup. Bake uncovered at 350° for 35 to 40 minutes or until browned. Serves 8.

# TATER TOT HAMBURGER CASSEROLE

1 1/2 lbs. hamburger
1 pkg. onion soup mix
3 eggs
10 soda crackers, crushed
1 (10 3/4 oz.) can cream of celery soup
1 (10 3/4 oz.) can cream of mushroom soup
1 cup of sour cream
1 (32 oz.) pkg. tater tots, thawed

Mix together hamburger, soup mix, eggs and cracker crumbs, press into bottom of a greased baking dish. Mix together soups and sour cream. Spread on top of meat. Stand tater tots side by side in rows. Cover loosely with foil and bake at 350° for 45 minutes. Remove foil and continue to bake 20 minutes longer. Serves 6.

# MEATBALLS AND POTATO SCALLOP

1 (5.12 oz.) can evaporated milk
1 egg, beaten
1 1/2 lbs. ground beef
3/4 cup cracker crumbs
1 tsp. dry mustard
1 1/2 tsp. salt
1/8 tsp. pepper
1/4 cup chopped onion
1/2 cup diced green pepper
8 medium peeled and sliced potatoes
1 soup can of milk
2 (10 3/4 oz.) cans cream of celery soup
chili sauce

Combine evaporated milk, egg, beef, cracker crumbs, seasonings, onion and green pepper, mix well and shape into balls. Cook potatoes in boiling water for 8 minutes or until partially done, drain. Spread potatoes in a large baking dish. Combine milk with soup, pour over potatoes. Arrange meatballs on top, brush with chili sauce. Bake at 350° for 45 minutes or until done. Serves 6 to 8.

# MEAT AND TATER TREAT

1 lb. ground beef
2 (10 3/4 oz.) cans cream of chicken soup
1 (10 oz.) pkg. frozen peas
1 (14 oz.) pkg. frozen tater tots
1/2 cup milk
1 (2.8 oz.) can of onion rings

Press ground beef into a square casserole. Add 1 can of soup over meat, pour peas over top. Place tater tots on peas. Add 1 can of soup, mixed with milk over tater tots. Place onion rings over top of mixture. Cover and bake 350° for 1 hour. Serves 4 to 6.

# CHEESEBURGER POTATO PIE

1 lb. ground beef
1 cup soft bread crumbs
1 small minced onion
1 tsp. salt
1/8 tsp. pepper
2/3 cup evaporated milk
1 1/2 cups grated Cheddar cheese
1/2 cup sour cream
4 medium potatoes, cooked, mashed and seasoned
paprika

Mix first 6 ingredients together, press into a greased 9 inch pie pan. Bake for 30 minutes at 350°. Remove from oven, drain. Sprinkle cheese over meat mixture. Mix sour cream with potatoes, spread over cheese. Sprinkle with paprika. Bake 15 minutes longer. Serves 6.

# HAMBURGER HAY STACKS

2 eggs
seasoned salt to taste
1 1/2 lbs. lean hamburger
3 cups shredded hash browns
3 Tbs. grated onion
3 Tbs. butter
1/4 cup catsup
1 1/2 cups shredded Cheddar cheese

In a bowl, mix eggs and seasoned salt with hamburger, shape into 6 patties. In a skillet brown patties. Remove and place in a baking dish. In a skillet, brown hash browns and onion in butter. Spread each patty with catsup, divide hash browns evenly over patties. Sprinkle with cheese. Bake at 350° for 10 to 15 minutes or until cheese is melted. Serves 6.

# POTATO PIZZA

1 (32 oz.) pkg. frozen shredded hash browns, thawed
1 (10 3/4 oz.) can Cheddar cheese soup
1 egg
1 tsp. salt
1/2 tsp. pepper
1 lb. ground beef or 1 lb. bulk sausage
2 Tbs. minced onion
1 (15 1/2 oz.) can pizza sauce
2 cups shredded Cheddar cheese
1 1/2 cup grated Mozzarella cheese
1 (4.4 oz.) can sliced ripe olives
1 (8 oz.) can sliced mushrooms, drained

In a large bowl, mix together hash browns, soup, egg, salt and pepper. Spread potato mixture over a large pizza pan. Bake in 450° oven for 20 to 25 minutes. In a skillet, cook ground beef and onions, drain fat. Stir in pizza sauce and simmer 5 minutes. Sprinkle Cheddar cheese over the baked potato crust. Spoon meat mixture over cheese and top with Mozzarella cheese, olive slices and mushrooms. Bake 5 minutes longer. Serves 6.

# MASHED POTATO PIZZA

## Crust

1 pkg. active dry yeast
1 cup warm water
1 1/2 cups flour
1 Tbs. oil
1 tsp. salt
2 cups sifted flour

Soften yeast in warm water. Beat in flour, stir in oil and salt. Mix in 2 cups flour, knead on lightly floured board for 8 minutes. Place in lightly greased bowl, turn to bring greased side up. Cover and let rise in a warm place until more than doubled, about 1 1/2 hours. Punch down, cover, and place in refrigerator until cold. Divide dough in half. On lightly floured surface roll each in a 12 inch circle. Place on pizza pans turning edge of dough up slightly. Brush each crust with 1 Tbs. oil.

## Filling

5 cups stiff mashed potatoes
1 tsp. salt
2 cups sour cream
2 Tbs. butter
pizza sauce

Whip first 4 ingredients together until fluffy. Spread potato mixture over each pizza crust. Gently spread pizza sauce over potato mixture.

## Topping

1 lb. cooked ground beef, 1 lb. sliced and cooked Italian sausage, sliced olives, chopped onions, chopped green peppers, sliced mushrooms, grated Mozzarella cheese, Parmesan cheese, grated Cheddar cheese.

Any of these toppings may be used. Bake at 400° for 18 minutes or until crust is done. Sprinkle with Parmesan cheese. 2 pizzas.

# CHEESE POTATO PIE

1 unbaked 9 inch pastry shell
2 cups cooked mashed potatoes
1/2 cup cream
1 Tbs. butter
1 cup cream style cottage cheese
1/2 cup sour cream
2 eggs
3/4 tsp. salt
1/8 tsp. garlic powder
1/8 tsp. pepper
1 3/4 cups shredded Swiss cheese
1/2 cup chopped onion
8 slices of bacon, cooked crisp, drained, and crumbled

Bake pie shell in preheated oven at 400° for about 8 minutes, or until nearly done. Remove from oven. In a bowl, combine mashed potatoes, cream, and butter, set aside. In a mixing bowl combine cottage cheese, sour cream, eggs, and seasonings, beat with electric mixer till smooth. Add potato mixture, beat 1 minute longer. Stir in Swiss cheese, onion, and bacon. Pour into warm shell. Bake 400° for 40 to 45 minutes or until golden brown. Serves 6.

# SAUSAGE POTATO AU GRATIN

1 (5.5 oz.) pkg. au gratin potato mix
1 (15.4 oz.) can green beans, drained
1 ( 8 oz.) pkg. brown and serve sausage links

In a 2 quart casserole prepare potato mix, following package directions. Stir in green beans. Place sausage links on top. Bake in preheated oven at 400° for 35 minutes or until potatoes are tender. Let stand a few minutes before serving. Serves 4.

# POTATO SAUSAGE LOAF

2 cups grated raw potatoes
1/2 lb. ground pork
1 lb. ground beef
1 medium grated onion
2 eggs, beaten
1/4 tsp. pepper
1/4 tsp. allspice
1 1/4 tsp. salt

In a bowl, mix first 8 ingredients together, Place in a casserole, cover. Bake at 350° for 1 hour. Serve hot with horseradish sauce. Serves 4.

### Horseradish Sauce

3/4 cup catsup
1 Tbs. Worcestershire sauce
2 Tbs. horseradish
1 Tbs. grated onion

Mix together all ingredients.

# ITALIAN BEEF AND POTATO CASSEROLE

1 lb. lean ground beef
1/2 tsp. oregano
1/4 tsp. basil
1/2 tsp. salt
1/8 tsp. garlic powder
1 (16 oz.) can tomatoes
1/2 cup water
1 (5 1/2 oz.) pkg. scalloped potatoes
1 (10 1/2 oz.) can pizza sauce
1 cup cubed Mozzarella cheese
1/2 cup grated Parmesan cheese

In a skillet brown meat until crumbly, drain. In a slow cooking pot, combine beef with next 8 ingredients. Cover and cook on low for 5 hours. Turn control to high. Stir in cheese cubes. Top with Parmesan cheese, cover and cook on high 10 to 15 minutes. Serves 4 to 6.

# STUFFED PEPPERS

1 lb. bulk sausage
1 medium chopped onion
2 large potatoes, cooked and diced
1 1/2 cups cubed bread
2 eggs, beaten
1 tsp. salt
1/2 tsp. pepper
1 tsp. ground sage
enough water to moisten
2 quarts water
6 large green peppers
1 (4 oz.) can tomato sauce
1 can water
2 cups grated medium Cheddar cheese

In a skillet, cook sausage and onion until browned. Remove from heat, add potatoes, bread crumbs, beaten eggs, salt, pepper and sage, mix well, add water to moisten. In a sauce pan bring 2 quarts of water to a boil. Scoop out and discard insides of green peppers. Cook pepper in boiling water until tender, but firm. Remove from water and drain. Fill peppers with filling, place in a baking dish. In a small bowl, add tomato sauce and water together, pour over peppers. Sprinkle peppers with grated cheese. Bake at 350° for 45 minutes. Serves 6.

# CREAMED FRENCH FRY CASSEROLE

1 (32 oz.) pkg. French fries, thawed
3 Tbs. margarine
1/2 cup chopped celery
3 Tbs. flour
1 1/2 cups milk
2 (10 3/4 oz.) cans cream celery soup
4 Tbs. minced onion
2 (2.5 oz.) pkg. dried beef, slivered
snipped parsley

Place French fries in a large baking dish. Sauté celery in margarine 2 to 3 minutes, stirring constantly. Blend in flour and add milk, cook until thickened and bubbly. Add soup, onion and dried beef, pour over French fries. Bake in preheated oven 350° for 35 minutes. Garnish with snipped parsley. Serves 6.

# BEEF AND POTATO SCALLOP

4 medium sized potatoes, peeled and cubed
1 1/2 cups shredded dried beef
1 1/2 Tbs. minced green onion
1 1/2 Tbs. minced green pepper
4 Tbs. margarine or butter
1 tsp. celery salt
1/8 tsp. pepper
4 Tbs. flour
2 cups milk
1 1/2 cups grated Cheddar cheese

In a 2 1/2 quart casserole mix together potatoes and dried beef. Add onions and green pepper. In a sauce pan heat margarine, add celery salt, pepper and flour, blend. Add milk and stir, cook until bubbly. Add 3/4 cup of cheese to the sauce, stirring until cheese is melted. Mix cheese sauce to potato mixture. Top with remaining cheese. Bake at 350° for 1 hour or until potatoes are done. 4 to 6 servings.

# SAUSAGE POTATO DINNER

4 cups potatoes, peeled and thinly sliced
2 (10 3/4 oz.) cans cream of celery soup
1/3 cup water
1 cup grated Cheddar cheese
1 lb. smoked sausage, cut into bite sized pieces
1/2 cup chopped green pepper
3 Tbs. minced onion

Butter a 10 inch baking dish. Line bottom with potatoes. In a sauce pan, heat soup and water, stirring until smooth. Stir in cheese until melted. Add sausage pieces, onion and green pepper. Pour over potatoes and bake at 350° for 1 hour or until potatoes are done. Serves 4.

# CREAMED POTATOES WITH SAUSAGE RING

8 medium potatoes, peeled and chunked into fourths
1 cup sliced celery
2 medium diced onions
1 tsp. salt
water
1 cup smoked sausage ring, sliced into 1/2 inch chunks
milk
1 cup milk
1/2 cup flour
1/8 tsp. pepper
1/2 tsp. salt

In a large sauce pan, add potatoes, celery, onions, salt and enough water to cover, cook until tender, but not mushy, drain. Add sausage slices and enough milk to cover potatoes. Bring to scald, but not boiling. Put into blender, milk, flour, pepper, and salt. Blend until smooth. Add slowly into potatoes, stirring continuously, until thickened. Frankfurters may be used in place of sausage. Serves 6.

# POTATO CABBAGE HOT DISH

3 lbs. shredded cabbage
1 1/2 lbs. ground beef
1 1/2 tsp. salt
1/4 tsp. pepper
3 cups canned tomatoes
3 Tbs. grated onion
4 cups seasoned mashed potatoes

Place cabbage in a buttered baking dish. In a skillet, brown ground beef, add salt and pepper. Place on top of cabbage. Pour tomatoes over meat mixture. Bake 325° for 1 hour. In a bowl mix onion and mashed potato together, spread over vegetables and meat. Bake 15 minutes longer. Serves 8.

# SAUCY HAM AND POTATO BAKE

3 Tbs. chopped onion
1/4 cup margarine
1/4 cup flour
1 tsp. salt
1 tsp. dry mustard
dash of pepper
1 1/4 cups milk
2 cups shredded Cheddar cheese
6 cups cooked sliced potatoes
2 cups diced ham

In a skillet, sauté onion in margarine. Blend in flour and seasonings. Add milk, cook, stirring constantly until thickened. Add 1 1/2 cups cheese, stir until melted. Mix potatoes into cheese sauce. Pour into a 2 quart casserole, reserving 1 cup potato slices. Arrange ham and remaining potato slices on top of casserole. Bake at 350° for 30 minutes. Top with remaining cheese. Serves 8.

# HAM AND POTATO BAKE

1/4 cup chopped onion
4 slices bacon, cooked crisp and crumbled
1/4 cup bacon drippings
1/4 cup flour
1 tsp. salt
1/8 tsp. pepper
1 1/2 cups milk
2 cups shredded medium Cheddar cheese
6 cups cooked potatoes, peeled and sliced
2 cups chopped ham
3 Tbs. pimiento

In a skillet, sauté onion in bacon drippings, blend in flour and seasonings, gradually add milk. Cook and stir constantly until thickened. Add 1 1/2 cups cheese and stir until melted. Mix potatoes, ham and pimiento in cheese sauce. Pour into casserole, top with remaining cheese and bacon pieces. Bake 350° for 30 minutes. Serves 8.

# PORK CHOP POTATO CASSEROLE

1 pkg. scalloped potato mix
1 (10 oz.) pkg. frozen peas
4 pork chops
salt and pepper

In a buttered 2 quart casserole place scalloped potatoes, prepared according to directions on package. Stir in peas. Season pork chops with salt and pepper, place over potato mixture. Bake uncovered at 325° for 65 to 70 minutes. Serves 4.

# HAM AND POTATO PIE
# WITH SOUR CREAM CRUST

## Crust

2 cups flour
1 tsp. salt
3/4 cup butter
1 egg
1/2 cup sour cream

Measure flour and salt into a bowl. Cut in butter until it resembles bread crumbs. Combine egg and sour cream. Stir into flour mixture, this makes a stiff dough. Divide dough into 2 parts. Roll each to make 14 x 6 inch rectangle. Place 1 crust on baking sheet.

## Filling

2 cups grated cooked potato
3 cups ground cooked ham
2 Tbs. grated onion
1 (4.5 oz.) can sliced mushrooms with juice
3/4 cup grated Swiss cheese
milk

In a bowl, combine first 5 ingredients. Arrange down the center of dough. Place top crust over the filling. Moisten the edges of crust and seal well. Make 3 or 4 small 1/2 inch slits in top to let the steam escape. Brush the pie with milk. Bake at 375° for 25 minutes or until golden brown. Cut into slices and serve hot. Serves 6.

# TATER TOT HAM CASSEROLE

1 (32 oz.) pkg. frozen tater tots, thawed
3 cups ground ham
3/4 cup thinly sliced celery
2 Tbs. butter
1/4 cup grated onion
1 cup sour cream
1/2 cup mayonnaise
2 tsp. lemon juice
2 (10 3/4 oz.) cans cream of celery soup
1 1/2 cups grated Cheddar cheese

In a large baking dish place tater tots. Layer ground ham over tater tots. In a small skillet sauté celery in butter, mix together with next 5 ingredients, pour over tater tots. Sprinkle cheese over the top. Bake at 350° for 45 to 50 minutes. Serves 8.

# POTATO HAM CROQUETTES

2 cups hot mashed potatoes
1 Tbs. melted butter
3 egg yolks
1 cup grated ham
2 cups cornflake crumbs
2 eggs, beaten

In a bowl, mix potatoes, butter and 2 egg yolks, beat until smooth. In a small sauce pan, over low heat, cook ham with remaining yolk until thickened, chill. Take a rounded tablespoon of potato mixture and make a hole in center, take a rounded teaspoon of ham mixture and fill center of potato. Close the hole and form a ball. Roll potato ball in corn flake crumbs, dip into beaten eggs then roll back into corn flake crumbs. Fry in hot oil, 380°, about 5 minutes, turning once, drain. About 10 to 12 croquetts.

# NEW POTATOES WITH GREEN BEANS

3 lbs. of fresh green beans, snapped
1 lb. of bacon (cut into pieces)
8 medium new potatoes, peeled and quartered
1 medium chopped onion
salt to taste

In a large heavy kettle, simmer beans in enough water to barely cover, until tender. Sauté bacon in a skillet. Add potatoes, onion, and bacon to the beans. Add salt to taste. Cover and continue to simmer until potatoes are done. New red potatoes may be used also. Serves 8.

# BROCCOLI POTATO SCALLOP

8 medium potatoes, cooked, peeled and cubed
1 (1 lb.) pkg. frozen broccoli
1 (8 oz.) large can mushroom pieces, with juice
3 Tbs. chopped green onion
1 (10 3/4 oz.) can cream of celery soup
1 (10 3/4 oz.) can cream of chicken soup
6 slices bacon, cooked crisp and crumbled
1 egg
1 cup sour cream
1 1/2 cups grated medium Cheddar cheese

Toss together potatoes and broccoli. Pour mixture into a large buttered baking dish. In a bowl mix next 7 ingredients, pour over potato mixture. Bake at 350° for 45 minutes or until bubbly and lightly browned. Top with cheese, return to oven for 5 to 10 minutes or until cheese is melted. Serves 8.

# SKILLET TATER PIE

6 slices chopped bacon
4 cups shredded hash browns
3 Tbs. grated onion
1 clove garlic, crushed
3 Tbs. finely chopped green pepper
3/4 cup shredded Cheddar cheese
1 tsp. salt
1/2 tsp. cumin
1/4 tsp. oregano
1/8 tsp. pepper
3 Tbs. milk
salsa, sour cream, sliced olives and grated cheese

In a skillet, over medium heat, cook bacon until lightly browned. Add next 9 ingredients, cook, stirring often for 10 minutes. Press mixture down into skillet with a mixing spoon. Sprinkle the milk evenly over the mixture, cover. Cook over low heat for 10 minutes. Loosen carefully and turn out onto serving platter, slice into 6 wedges. Top with salsa, sour cream, olives and cheese.

# PRAIRIE SKILLET SUPPER

4 large thinly sliced potatoes
3 sliced carrots
1/2 cup sliced celery
3 Tbs. chopped onion
3 Tbs. vegetable oil
1 tsp. salt
dash of pepper
1 smoked sausage link, cut into 1 inch slices

In a heavy skillet, over medium heat, brown sliced potatoes, carrots, celery, and onion in oil. Add salt and pepper. When tender, place sausage link chunks on top of potatoes. Cover and heat 20 minutes. Serves 4.

# SALMON POTATO LOAF

1 1/2 cups drained salmon
1 1/2 cups mashed potatoes
1 tsp. salt
1 medium grated onion
3 eggs, separated
2 Tbs. snipped parsley
2 Tbs. melted butter

In a bowl, mix salmon, potato, salt, onion, egg yolks and parsley. Beat egg whites until stiff. Fold into mixture. Place in a well buttered baking dish. Pour melted butter over top. Bake at 350° for 35 to 40 minutes. Serves 4.

# POTATO TUNA PATTIES

2 cups mashed potatoes
1 (6 oz.) can of tuna, drained and flaked
2 eggs, beaten
2 Tbs. grated onion
1/2 cup flour
1 tsp. baking powder

In a bowl, mix all ingredients together and make into patties. Lightly flour both sides of patties. Brown on oiled griddle until golden brown. Makes about 8 patties.

# COD FISH PUFFS WITH COCKTAIL SAUCE

1 cup flaked cod fish
3 cups diced potatoes
2 Tbs. milk
2 Tbs. butter
1/8 tsp. pepper
2 eggs, beaten

In a sauce pan, simmer fish and potatoes together until potatoes are tender. Drain well, mash and add remaining ingredients. Beat until light and fluffy. Drop by tablespoonful into hot oil at 380° until brown. Serve with cocktail sauce. Makes about 30 puffs.

### Cocktail Sauce

4 tsp. horseradish
1/2 cup catsup
1/2 tsp. salt
1 tsp. celery salt
2 Tbs. vinegar
6 Tbs. lemon juice
1/2 tsp. Tabasco sauce
2 tsp. Worcestershire sauce

In a bowl, mix all ingredients well, chill.

# TUNA POTATO CASSEROLE

3 cups cooked sliced potatoes
1 (15.4 oz.) can drained peas
1 (6 oz.) can drained tuna
1/4 cup minced onion
2 (10 3/4 oz.) cans cream of mushroom soup
1 1/2 cups grated medium Cheddar cheese

Layer ingredients in order listed in a 2 quart casserole. Bake 375° for 30 minutes or until done. 6 servings.

# POTATO SAUERKRAUT BAKE

8 medium potatoes, cooked with skins, peeled and cubed
1 Polish or German sausage link, sliced
1 (32 oz.) jar of sauerkraut
1 cup mayonnaise
1 cup milk

Place potatoes in bottom of a Dutch oven. Layer Polish or German sausage over potatoes. In a mixing bowl, mix together sauerkraut, mayonnaise and milk. Pour over potatoes. Bake 45 minutes at 350°. Serves 8.

# POTATO CORN SCALLOP

1 (32 oz.) pkg. tater tots, thawed
6 slices bacon
2 Tbs. chopped green pepper
1/3 cup sliced celery
2 Tbs. chopped onion
2 Tbs. chopped pimiento
1 (15.4 oz.) can creamed corn
1 (15.4 oz.) can whole kernel corn, drained
2 (10 3/4 oz.) cans cream of celery soup
2 Tbs. melted butter
1 cup dried bread crumbs

Place tater tots in a large buttered baking dish. Cut bacon into small pieces. Sauté bacon, green pepper, celery, onion and pimiento until crispy tender, drain. Add corn and celery soup to mixture. Pour over potatoes. Toss bread crumbs and butter together and sprinkle over scallop. Bake 35 to 40 minutes in preheated 350° oven. Serves 6 to 8.

# TATER TOT CHICKEN BAKE

1 (2 lb.) pkg. frozen tater tots
2 cups cooked diced chicken
1 cup frozen peas
2 (10 3/4 oz.) cans cream of chicken soup
1 (10 3/4 oz.) can cream of celery soup
1/2 cup milk
1 egg, slightly beaten
1/2 tsp. salt

Place tater tots in a large buttered baking dish, spread diced chicken evenly over tots. Sprinkle peas over chicken. In a bowl mix together soups, milk, egg and salt, pour over peas and cover. Bake at 350° for 35 to 40 minutes. Remove from oven and let set for 5 minutes before serving. Serves 8.

# TURKEY POTATO PIE

2 (10 inch) pastry shells
5 baked potatoes
1 cup sour cream
1 1/2 tsp. Mrs. Dash's seasoning
1/4 cup melted butter
1 tsp. garlic powder
4 cups cooked diced turkey
1 egg

Roll out pie shells. Scoop potatoes from skins into bowl, add next 5 ingredients, mix gently. Place first pastry shell on cookie sheet, mound filling in center leaving a 3/4 inch border, place second shell over the mixture and bring the edges of top and bottom shell together and seal. Beat egg and brush over the top crust. Make 3 or 4 slits in top of pie to allow the steam to escape. Bake at 400° for 25 to 35 minutes or until golden brown. Serves 6.

# HASH BROWNS WITH FRANKFURTER BAKE

1/2 cup milk
1 (10 3/4 oz.) can cream of celery soup
1/2 tsp. salt
1/2 tsp. dry mustard
1 (14 1/2 oz.) can green beans, drained
1 (15.4 oz.) cup canned French fried onions
1 (12 oz.) pkg. hash brown potatoes, thawed
5 frankfurters, sliced
1 1/2 cups shredded Cheddar cheese

In a 2 quart casserole mix together first 8 ingredients. Cover and bake at 350° for 45 to 50 minutes or until done. Remove from oven, sprinkle with cheese, return to oven bake until cheese melts. Serves 4.

# ONE DISH MEAL

1 (10 3/4 oz.) can cream of mushroom soup
1 (10 3/4 oz.) can cream of celery soup
1 cup of water
1 cup of milk
6 to 8 medium potatoes, peeled, sliced
1 Tbs. parsley flakes
dash of pepper
1/4 tsp. garlic powder
2 cups sliced frankfurters
sliced cheese

Place soups, water and milk in a large baking dish, stir well. Add potatoes, parsley, pepper, garlic powder, and, frankfurters cover. Bake 1 hour and 15 minutes at 350°, or until potatoes are tender. Uncover, place sliced cheese to cover top. Bake until cheese melts. Serves 6 to 8.

# FRANK HASH BROWN CASSEROLE

1 (10 3/4 0z.) can of cream of celery soup
1 (10 3/4 0z.) can of cream of chicken soup
1 cup canned French fried onions
1 (12 oz.) pkg. frozen hash brown potatoes, thawed
1/2 tsp. salt
dash of pepper
1/2 tsp. ground mustard
6 sliced frankfurters
1 cup French fried onions

In a buttered 2 quart casserole, stir together all ingredients, except 1/2 cup French fried onions. Cover and bake at 350° 50 minutes. Uncover and top with 1/2 cup French fried onions. Bake 15 minutes longer. Serves 4.

# POTATO STUFFED FRANKS

12 frankfurters
3 cups seasoned mashed potatoes
2 Tbs. grated onion
1 1/2 cups grated Cheddar cheese
paprika

Split frankfurters length-wise, lay cut side up in a buttered baking dish. In a mixing bowl, mix potatoes and onion together, spoon over frankfurters. Sprinkle with cheese and paprika. Bake 425° for 20 minutes. Serves 6.

# NORTH OF THE BORDER TACOS

3 medium grated potatoes
1 grated carrot
1 grated onion
1/2 grated green pepper
1 lb. ground beef
salt, garlic powder, pepper to taste
1/2 cup taco sauce
tortillas
grated cheese
sliced tomatoes
chopped lettuce

In a skillet, mix first 5 ingredients with spices and brown. Add taco sauce, simmer 15 minutes. Drop tortillas on oiled griddle for 2 seconds, on each side. Fill with meat mixture, cheese, tomatoes, and lettuce. Pour hot sauce over top if desired. 10 to 15 tacos.

## HASH TACOS

1 (15 oz.) can of corned beef hash
1 cup raw tomatoes, seeded and diced
1 cup chopped green pepper
3 Tbs. chopped onion
taco shells
shredded lettuce
grated Cheddar cheese
taco sauce

Heat hash in skillet. Add tomatoes, green peppers, onions and mix thoroughly. Spoon into heated taco shells. Garnish with lettuce, cheese and taco sauce. 8 to 10 tacos.

# MEAT AND POTATO TACOS

1 lb. ground beef
2 cups hash browns
1/3 cup chopped onion
1 (4.5 oz.) can chopped olives
1 envelope taco seasoning mix
1 1/2 cups drained canned tomatoes
12 taco shells
shredded lettuce
sour cream
taco sauce

     In a skillet, combine ground beef, olives, hash browns, and onion. Cook until done. Stir in seasoning and tomatoes. Cook uncovered 5 minutes. Heat taco shells. Spoon mixture into shells. Top with lettuce, sour cream and cheese. Add taco sauce if desired. 12 tacos.

# HASH

1 1/2 cups beef broth
2 cups ground roast beef
2 cups chopped cooked potato
1/2 cup grated onion
2 tsp. salt
1/2 tsp. pepper
1 Tbs. Worcestershire sauce
1/2 cup bread crumbs
2 Tbs. melted margarine

     Mix first 7 ingredients in a 2 quart casserole. In a bowl, toss bread crumbs and melted margarine together, sprinkle over casserole. Bake at 350° for 45 minutes or until heated through. Serves 4.

# ENGLISH HASH

4 cups chopped cabbage
1/2 cup finely chopped onion
1/2 cup finely chopped green pepper
1/4 cup cooking oil
2 cups finely diced cooked potatoes
1 1/2 cups ground cooked roast beef
2/3 cup gravy, canned or leftover
salt and pepper to taste

In a sauce pan, cook cabbage in boiling salted water, drain. In a large skillet, cook onion and green pepper in oil until tender. Mix drained cabbage, potatoes, meat, gravy, salt and pepper, stir into onion and green pepper. Press firmly into same skillet, cook until crust forms. Invert on platter. Cut in wedges. Serves 4 to 6

# MEXICAN HASH

2 cups ground roast beef
1/2 cup chopped onion
2 Tbs. oil
2 cups finely chopped raw potatoes
1 (12 oz.) can drained whole kernel corn
1 (4.5 oz.) chopped mild chili peppers
1 (10 3/4 oz.) can tomato soup

In a skillet, cook beef and onion in oil until tender. Add potatoes, corn, chilies, and tomato soup, mix. Cover, bake at 350° for 40 minutes. Serves 4

# HASH BURGERS

1 (15 oz. can corned beef hash
2 Tbs. finely chopped onions
2 Tbs. finely chopped dill pickle
1 Tbs. prepared mustard
1 Tbs. finely chopped jalapeno pepper
1/3 cup mayonnaise
6 slices sharp American cheese
3 hamburger buns, split and toasted

Cut corned beef hash into 6 slices, place on a ungreased baking sheet. Broil on top rack for 5 minutes. Combine onion, pickle, mustard, peppers and mayonnaise, spread on hash slices. Place cheese slice on top of each hash slice. Return to broiler until cheese begins to melt. Place on toasted bun halves. Makes 6 open-faced sandwiches.

# HOT CHICKEN POTATO DISH

3 cups cooked sliced potatoes
2 cups cooked diced chicken breasts
1 cup diced celery
6 eggs, boiled and chopped
1/3 cup chopped onion
1 tsp. salt
1 1/2 cups mayonnaise
2 (10 3/4 oz.) cans cream of chicken soup
1 1/2 cups grated American cheese

Mix all ingredients except cheese in a large baking pan. Cover and bake at 350° for 40 minutes. Remove cover and top with cheese, return to oven for 5 minutes until cheese is melted. Serves 6.

# FILLED POTATO DUMPLINGS

## Dumplings

2 cups cold, seasoned potatoes
1 egg yolk
1/4 cup flour
1 quart of water

## Filling

1 cup finely grated ham
1/4 tsp. allspice
1 Tbs. minced onion

Combine potato, egg yolk, flour, in a bowl, mix well. In another bowl combine ham, allspice and onion, mix well. Divide potato mixture into 8 parts. Press about 1 Tbs. ham mixture into center of each dumpling. Seal completely within the potato dumpling. Chill over night or freeze before cooking. To cook dumplings, bring water to a boil with 1 Tbs. salt. Reduce heat so the water is simmering. Drop in 1 to 3 dumplings, simmer for 10 minutes. Do not boil as the dumplings will break. Remove from water with slotted spoon to a hot dish. Keep hot and repeat until all dumplings are cooked. 1 quart of chicken broth may be used instead of water.

# POTATO DUMPLINGS

3 cups mashed potatoes
2 Tbs. butter
2 eggs
1 tsp. salt
dash of pepper
1 1/2 tsp. baking powder
enough flour to make a stiff dough

In a bowl, mix together the first 6 ingredients. Add flour to the potato mixture gradually until dough is stiff. Drop by heaping teaspoonfuls into hot broth. Cook 3 to 5 minutes.

# QUICK POTATO DUMPLINGS IN SAUERKRAUT

1 cup potato flakes
1 cup boiling water
1 1/2 tsp. salt
2 eggs
1 cup flour
2 cups water
1 can sauerkraut

In a bowl, combine potato flakes, boiling water and salt, mix well. Cool, add eggs and mix well, add flour. In a sauce pan add the water to a can of sauerkraut, bring to boil. Drop dumplings by spoonfuls into boiling sauerkraut, cover and cook for 15 minutes.

# POTATO CRUST

Instant mashed potatoes, enough for 2 servings
1 1/2 cups flour
2 tsp. baking powder
1/2 tsp. salt
1/3 cup shortening
1/4 cup milk or water

Prepare potatoes as directed on package, cool. In a bowl measure flour, baking powder and salt. Cut potatoes and shortening into flour mixture thoroughly. Stir in milk or water. Roll dough into a ball and place on floured cloth covered board. Sprinkle with flour and roll dough into the shape of your casserole. Place over favorite meat pie filling. Crimp edges and cut slits in dough to allow steam to escape. Bake 350° 45 minutes or until crust is brown.

# POTATO STUFFING

8 slices bacon, chopped
1 cup chopped celery
1 cup chopped onion
2 tsp. thyme
1 tsp. sage
1/4 tsp. pepper
4 cups diced cooked potatoes
2 eggs
1 (10 3/4 oz.) can golden mushroom soup
1 soup can of water
5 cups cubed stuffing mix

In a sauce pan, brown bacon, add celery, onion and seasonings, cook until tender. Add remaining ingredients, toss lightly. Spoon into a 2 quart buttered casserole. Bake at 350° for 45 minutes. May be used to stuff 12 to 15 pound turkey.

# POTATO PATTIES

2 cups mashed potatoes
1 1/2 tsp. baking powder
1/2 tsp. salt
2 Tbs. grated onion
2 eggs
2/3 cup flour

Mix all ingredients well. Measure 1/3 cup mixture for each patty. Roll in flour and flatten. Place on well oiled hot grill or skillet. Brown on both sides. Use medium high heat. Makes 8 to 10 patties.

Crumbled bacon pieces and 1 cup drained whole kernel corn may be added.

# HAM POTATO PATTIES

4 cups shredded cooked potatoes
3 Tbs. minced onion
1 1/2 cups ground ham
2 eggs
1 tsp. dry mustard
3/4 tsp. salt
1/2 cu. flour

In a bowl, mix together all ingredients, make into 12 patties. On a well buttered hot grill, brown patties on both sides.

# CHEESE TOPPED POTATO PATTIES

frozen hash brown patties
finely chopped bell pepper
finely chopped onion
bacon, cooked crisp and crumbled
ground ham
grated cheese

Grill frozen hash brown patties until golden brown on both sides. Top with any of the above ingredients. Sprinkle with cheese, heat until cheese melts.

# VEGGIE POTATO NESTS

2 cups mashed potatoes
1 egg, separated
2 cups mixed vegetables, cooked and drained
3 tsp. grated onion
1 cup shredded sharp processed American cheese

In a bowl, mix potato and egg yolk. Form into 4 nests on baking sheet. Beat egg white and brush over potatoes. Mix vegetables and onion. Divide and put into potato nests. Sprinkle with cheese. Bake at 375° for 30 minutes or until lightly browned. Serves 4.

# GRAVIES AND SAUCES

## HAMBURGER GRAVY

2 Tbs. oil
1/2 lb. hamburger
4 Tbs. flour
2 cups milk
1 tsp. salt
dash of pepper

In a skillet heat oil, brown hamburger. Blend flour into meat. Add milk, salt and pepper, cook and stir until thickened and bubbly. Serve over hash browns, mashed or baked potatoes. Serves 4.

## SAUSAGE GRAVY

1 Tbs. butter
1/2 lb. bulk sausage
4 Tbs. flour
2 cups milk

In a skillet, brown sausage in butter. Blend flour with sausage and brown. Add milk and season to taste. Stir until thickened. Serve over hash browns, mashed or baked potato. Serves 4.

## MUSHROOM OR CHICKEN SAUCE

1 cup milk
2 envelopes cream of mushroom or cream of chicken cup-a-soup
2/3 cup shredded American cheese

In a small sauce pan, heat milk to scalding, add mushroom or chicken soup mix and cheese. Remove from heat. Serve over potatoes. Makes 1 1/2 cups.

# RICH SHRIMP SAUCE

5 Tbs. butter or margarine
1/3 cup minced celery
1/4 cup minced onion
4 Tbs. flour
1 cup milk
1 cup half & half cream
1/2 tsp. salt
dash of pepper
2 (6 oz.) cans shrimp, drained
1 Tbs. lemon juice

  In a skillet over medium heat, melt butter. Add celery and onion. Sauté until tender. Blend in flour and stir. Add milk, cream, salt and pepper. Stir until thickened and bubbly. Add shrimp and lemon juice, heat. May be served over mashed potatoes, baked potato, or hash browns. Serves 4.

# BAKED POTATOES AND TOPPINGS

## MICROWAVE BAKED POTATOES

Using 6 to 9 oz. potatoes each, pierce with fork three to four times. Place on floor of microwave oven on a paper towel about 1 inch apart. Bake:

| | | | |
|---|---|---|---|
| 1 potato | 6 | to | 8 minutes |
| 2 potatoes | 8 | to | 10 minutes |
| 3 potatoes | 10 | to | 14 minutes |
| 4 potatoes | 14 | to | 18 minutes |
| 5 potatoes | 18 | to | 22 minutes |

Potatoes may still feel firm when done, let stand to soften or may wrap in foil to keep hot.

For drier skins on microwave baked potatoes, stand pierced potatoes on end in microwave proof muffin pan. Bake according to directions.

## BAKED POTATOES WITH TOPPINGS

Scrub 8 to 10 ounce potatoes. Pierce the skin of each potato with a fork 3 or 4 times to allow steam to escape. Rub skin with oil, butter or bacon grease for a soft skin. May be baked in foil for a tender skin. Bake at 400° for 45 minutes to an hour.

### Toppings

1.   Butter or margarine
2.   Sour cream and chives
3.   8 oz. cream cheese, 1/3 cup sour cream, beaten fluffy. Add 1 1/2 tsp. lemon juice, 1/2 tsp. garlic salt, 1 Tbs. minced onion.
4.   Herb-garlic dressing with chopped fresh tomato, marinated artichoke hearts.
5.   Any or all of these: chopped green onion, grated cheese, crumbled bacon or chives.

# TWICE BAKED POTATOES

6 large potatoes scrubbed well and patted dry.
1/4 cup margarine
3/4 tsp. salt
1 cup sour cream
1 cup grated Cheddar cheese
paprika

Butter lightly. Pierce each to allow steam to escape. Place on baking sheet. Bake 1 hour and 15 minutes at 350° or until done. Remove from oven. Lay potato length-wise. Cut 3/4 inch off top. Carefully scoop the pulp from center, leaving skins whole. Put potato pulp into bowl. Beat potato pulp, margarine, salt and sour cream with an electric mixer. Fold in cheese. Scoop potato mixture into the potato skins. Place on baking sheet. Sprinkle with paprika. Bake 20 min. at 400°.

# BAKED POTATOES
# WITH BROCCOLI CHEESE SAUCE

4 medium baked potatoes
1 1/2 cups chopped broccoli
2 Tbs. butter
2 Tbs. flour
1 cup milk
1 cup shredded sharp Cheddar cheese

Follow the directions for baked potatoes. In a sauce pan, steam broccoli about 10 minutes in small amount of water over medium heat, drain. Melt butter in sauce pan, stir in flour. Add milk and stir until thickened. Add cheese, stirring until melted, add broccoli. Serve over the baked potatoes.

# THE POTATO DELUXE

Bake potatoes according to directions, cut open from end to end, and place in center of plate.

Top each potato with:

1/4 cup cooked ground beef
1 Tbs. canned sliced mushrooms
1/2 cup cheese sauce
1 Tbs. chopped or sliced olives
1 Tbs. chopped green onion
3 Tbs. shredded Cheddar cheese
2 Tbs. sour cream

Top sour cream with sprinkle of sunflower seeds and bacon bits. Garnish with tomato wedges on a lettuce leaf.

## Cheese Sauce

4 Tbs. margarine
4 Tbs. flour
2 cups milk
3/4 tsp. salt
1/2 tsp. pepper
1 1/2 cups cubed sharp Cheddar cheese

Melt margarine in sauce pan, add flour and blend. Add milk, salt, and pepper. Blend well. Add cheese. Cook on low heat until bubbly and cheese is melted. Makes about 3 cups.

# POLISH REUBEN POTATOES

1 (32 oz.) jar sauerkraut
2 cups sliced Polish sausages
1 (10 3/4 oz..) can cream of mushroom soup
5 baked potatoes

In a sauce pan simmer sauerkraut and Polish sausages for 10 minutes. Add mushroom soup, heat. Serve over baked potatoes.

# CHILI BAKED POTATOES

1 lb. ground beef
1 medium diced onion
1 tsp. salt
1/4 tsp. pepper
1 cup diced green pepper
2 Tbs. oil
1 Tbs. chili powder
1/2 cup tomato sauce
4 baked potatoes
1 cup grated Cheddar cheese

In a skillet, brown meat, onion and green pepper, salt and pepper in oil, drain. Add chili powder and tomato sauce. Cover and simmer for 5 minutes. Cut potatoes in half length-wise, scoop out pulp and mash. Put pulp and grated cheese back into shells, pour chili mix over potato halves.

# SLOPPY JOE TOPPED POTATOES

3/4 lb. ground beef
2 Tbs. grated onion
1 (15 oz.) can sloppy joe mix
1/3 cup water
1/2 cup sour cream
4 baked potatoes

In a small skillet, brown ground beef and onion, drain. Stir in sloppy joe mix and water, bring to a boil, reduce heat. Cover, simmer for 5 minutes. Stir in sour cream, heat through, but do not boil. Spoon over potatoes.

# HAMBURGER STUFFED POTATOES

6 large baked potatoes
1 (10 3/4 oz.) can Cheddar cheese soup
1 lb. hamburger, browned
1 small onion, chopped and browned
1/4 cup margarine
salt and pepper to taste
milk, enough to make fluffy
12 slices processed American cheese

Cut potatoes in half and scoop out pulp. In a large bowl, mix potatoes, soup, hamburger, onion, margarine, salt, pepper and milk. Fill potato skins with mixture. Top with a slice of cheese. Return to oven until hot and cheese is melted.

# HAMBURGER STROGANOFF
# TOPPED POTATOES

1 lb. ground beef
2 Tbs. butter
2 Tbs. flour
1 Tbs. minced onion
1/2 tsp. garlic salt
1/2 tsp. paprika
1 cup water, with 1 beef bouillon cube
1 (4.5 oz.) can sliced mushrooms with liquid
1 envelope of sour cream sauce mix
1 (6 oz.) can evaporated milk
6 baked potatoes

In a skillet, brown meat in butter, stir in flour and mix in next 6 ingredients, cover. Simmer 10 minutes. Combine sauce mix with milk, stir into meat mixture, heat through. Serve with baked potatoes.

# BAKED POTATO WITH HAM TOPPING

4 large baking potatoes
2 egg yolks, beaten
1/2 tsp. salt
3 Tbs. butter
2 cups sliced fresh mushrooms
1/4 cup minced onion
1/4 cup diced green pepper
1 Tbs. parsley flakes
2 Tbs. flour
1/2 cup milk
2 cups chopped ham
1 cup grated Cheddar cheese
paprika

Bake potatoes and cut in half, length-wise. Scoop pulp out and place in a bowl, leaving shell. Add egg yolks and salt to potatoes, whip until fluffy. In a skillet, melt butter, sauté mushrooms, onion, green pepper, and parsley. Blend flour in milk and add to mushroom mixture, stirring until thickened. Fill potato shells with whipped potato mixture, top with thickened sauce and chopped ham. Sprinkle grated cheese on top of each potato. Sprinkle with paprika. Bake at 350° for 20 minutes or until slightly browned on top.

# ONION STUFFED POTATOES

6 large baked potatoes
1 envelope onion mushroom soup mix
1/2 cup butter or margarine
milk

Split potatoes length-wise. Scoop pulp from shells and place in a bowl. Add soup mix, butter, and enough milk to potatoes to whip fluffy. Refill shells. Garnish with shredded Cheddar or American cheese, crumbled cooked bacon, chives, or buttered crumbs. Bake at 350° until heated through, about 20 minutes.

For sour cream potatoes use 1 cup sour cream in place of butter and cut the milk in half.

# HAM STUFFED POTATOES

6 large baked potatoes
1/2 cup chopped onion
1/2 cup chopped celery
2 Tbs. butter
2 cups diced cooked ham
1/4 tsp. garlic powder
1/4 tsp. salt
1/4 cup butter
1/4 cup flour
2 cups milk
1/4 cup salsa sauce
4 Tbs. fine dried bread crumbs
1 Tbs. melted butter

Half baked potatoes length-wise. Scoop out pulp and cube. Reserve potato shells. In a skillet, cook onion and celery in butter until tender. Add ham, garlic powder, and salt. Cover, simmer 10 minutes. In a sauce pan, melt butter, blend in flour. Add milk, cook and stir until thickened and bubbly. Add salsa sauce. Combine ham mixture and cubed potatoes. Spoon into potato shells. Arrange in baking dish. Mix bread crumbs and melted butter, sprinkle crumb mixture on top of stuffed potatoes. Bake at 350° for 30 minutes.

# STUFFED POTATOES

6 large potatoes
1 lb. ground beef
1 pkg. onion mushroom soup mix
1 (3 oz.) pkg. cream cheese
1 egg

Cut raw potatoes in two, length-wise. Scoop out center of potatoes, about 3/4 inch deep. In a skillet, cook ground beef, drain remove from heat. Add soup mix, cream cheese and egg, mix well. Scoop into cavity of potatoes. Fit potatoes back together, wrap tightly in foil. Bake at 350° for 1 hour and 15 minutes, or until tender. Serve plain or with sour cream.

# REGAL POTATO

4 large baked potatoes
1/4 cup chopped onion
1/4 cup chopped green pepper
1/4 cup chopped celery
2 cloves minced garlic
3 Tbs. butter or margarine
1 cup chopped fresh or frozen shrimp
1/2 cup sour cream
1 tsp. lemon juice
3/4 tsp. Worcestershire sauce
dash of hot pepper sauce
1/2 cup shredded mozzarella cheese
grated Parmesan cheese
1 Tbs. chopped green onion

Cut potato in half, length-wise. Scoop out pulp, leaving 1/4 inch shell, place in a bowl, mash. Place shells on baking sheet. In a skillet, cook onion, pepper, celery, and garlic in butter until tender. Add shrimp and cook 2 minutes longer. Remove from heat. In a mixing bowl, combine sour cream, juice, sauces, and Mozzarella cheese. Stir in mashed potato. Fill the shells with mixture. Sprinkle with Parmesan cheese and green onion. Bake at 350° for 20 to 25 minutes.

# GOLDEN BAKED POTATOES

5 mcdium potatocs, pcclcd
2 Tbs. melted margarine
1 1/2 cups cornflake crumbs
1 tsp. salt

Brush potatoes with margarine and coat with crumb and salt mixture. Arrange in unbuttered baking dish. Bake uncovered at 375° for 1 hour or until done.

# CRAB STUFFED POTATOES

4 large baked potatoes
2 Tbs. butter
1/3 cup milk
1/2 cup grated Cheddar cheese
1/8 tsp. pepper
1 (3 oz.) pkg. softened cream cheese
1 (7 oz.) can flaked crab
1 Tbs. minced chives
1/4 tsp. salt
melted butter
paprika and parsley

Cut a thin length-wise slice from the top of each baked potato. Carefully scoop out pulp, leaving 1/4 inch shells. In a bowl, whip potato pulp with next 8 ingredients until smooth and fluffy. Mound mixture into shells, packing lightly. Top with melted butter, paprika and parsley. Bake uncovered at 400° for 20 minutes or until heated thoroughly and lightly browned. Bake unthawed at 375° for 35 minutes.

# BLEU CHEESE AND BACON STUFFED POTATOES

3 medium baked potatoes
1/2 cup milk
3 Tbs. butter
3/4 tsp. salt
dash of pepper
6 Tbs. bleu cheese dressing
3 slices bacon, cooked crispy, drained
chopped green onions or chives

Cut slice from top of potatoes. Scoop out pulp and place in a bowl, mash. Add milk, butter, salt and pepper, beat until fluffy. Pile lightly into shells. Garnish each potato with 2 Tbs. bleu cheese dressing and 1 crumbled strip of bacon. Return to oven and heat for 5 minutes. Garnish each with chopped green onions or chives. Serve at once.

# TURKEY STUFFED POTATOES

2 large baked potatoes
2/3 cup sour cream
2/3 cup mayonnaise
1/2 cup grated parmesan cheese
1 small minced onion
 3/4 tsp. oregano
1/2 tsp. salt
1/4 tsp. pepper
2 cups cooked cubed turkey
2 Tbs. seasoned bread crumbs,

Cut potatoes in half, length-wise. Scoop pulp out, leaving a shell. In a bowl, mash potatoes, set aside. In medium bowl, mix sour cream, mayonnaise, cheese, onion, oregano, salt and pepper. Mix mashed potatoes and turkey into sour cream mixture. Place potato shells in shallow baking dish, fill with mixture. Sprinkle evenly with seasoned bread crumbs. Bake at 350° for 30 minutes.

## Seasoned Bread Crumbs

1/4 cup bread crumbs
1 1/2 tsp. Schillings vegetable seasoning
1 Tbs. melted butter
1/2 tsp. paprika

In a small bowl, toss all ingredients together.

# VEGGIE STUFFED POTATOES (MICROWAVE)

4 large baking potatoes
3/4 cup milk
1/4 cup butter or margarine
1 tsp. salt
1/8 tsp. pepper
1/2 cup frozen peas
1/2 cup shredded carrot
1 Tbs. finely chopped onion
1 Tbs. water
1 cup grated cheese

Pierce potatoes with a fork. Arrange at least 1 inch apart on paper towel Microwave on high for 12 to 18 minutes, or until slightly firm, rearranging and turning over after half the time. Cover with a heavy towel, let stand 5 to 10 minutes. Halve each baked potato length-wise, and scoop out pulp. Place in a bowl, mash with milk, butter, salt and pepper. In 1 quart casserole combine peas, carrots and onion in water, cover. Microwave on high 1 1/2 to 3 1/2 minutes or until tender. Drain, stir in mashed potatoes. Spoon mixture into shells. Place stuffed shells on waxed paper lined tray, freeze until firm. Wrap in 2 pkgs. and label and freeze no longer than 2 months. To serve unwrap 1 pkg. and place halves on serving plate. Cover with wax paper. Microwave on high 8 to 11 minutes, or until hot, rearranging 1 or 2 times. Sprinkle each half with 1 Tbs. cheese. Microwave on high 2 minutes or until cheese melts, rotating once during cooking time, let stand 3 minutes.

# SOUPS

## POTATO SOUP

8 medium potatoes, peeled and sliced
1 large chopped onion
2 cups milk
1 cup half and half cream
1 Tbs. butter
1 tsp. salt
dash of pepper
1 tsp. celery salt
parsley flakes

Prepare potatoes and onion, put into a deep sauce pan. Add enough water to just cover potatoes. Cover, bring to boil, lower heat and simmer until potatoes begin to mush. Add milk, half & half cream, butter and seasonings. Heat and serve. Parsley flakes may be added. Serves 6.

### Cream of Potato Soup

Make basic soup recipe and add: 1 can cream of mushroom soup and 1 can cream of celery soup. Serves 8.

### Potato Corn Soup

Make basic soup recipe, add: 2 cans celery soup and 1 can whole kernel corn, drained. 1/2 lb. bacon, diced and sautéed. Serves 8.

### Potato Ham Soup

Make basic soup recipe and add: 2 cups shredded medium or sharp Cheddar cheese, 2 cups diced ham Serves 8.

### Potato Chicken Soup

Make basic soup recipe and add: 1 can cream of celery soup, 1 can cream of chicken soup, 2 cups diced chicken. Serves 8.

# CREAMY POTATO SOUP

4 slices of bacon
3 medium potatoes
1/2 cup chopped onion
1/2 cup chopped carrots
1/2 cup chopped celery
4 cups milk
2 tsp. salt
1/4 tsp. pepper
1 cup sour cream
2 Tbs. flour
2 tsp. paprika

In a skillet, fry bacon until crisp, drain and reserve 3 Tbs. drippings. Add potatoes, onion, carrots and celery to drippings. Cover and cook slowly for about 20 minutes or until vegetables are tender. Combine milk, salt, pepper, sour cream, flour and paprika. Gradually add to vegetable mixture. Stir and cook until soup begins to bubble. Top with crumbled bacon. Serves 6 to 8.

# CREAM OF CARROT POTATO SOUP

4 medium potatoes
3 large carrots
1 medium onion
boiling salted water
2 Tbs. butter
2 Tbs. flour
1 cup canned milk
salt and pepper to taste

Peel and slice potatoes, carrots and onion. In a large sauce pan, cook until tender in enough salted boiling water to cover vegetables. Mash vegetables in liquid. Melt butter in a small skillet, stir in flour until bubbly. Add milk, stir until slightly thickened. Add to vegetable pulp, season with salt and pepper. Serves 4 to 6.

# POTATO PEA SOUP

1 (12 oz.) pkg. hash browns
2 cups water
2 Tbs. grated onion
1 cup half and half cream
1 (10 3/4 oz.) can split pea soup
1 (10 3/4 oz.) can cream of celery soup
1 cup ground ham
1/8 tsp. garlic powder
1/8 tsp. pepper

In a sauce pan, add hash browns, water and onion, cover and cook slowly until tender. Add remaining ingredients. Heat and simmer 10 minutes. Serves 6.

# CREAM OF POTATO TOMATO SOUP

4 to 6 slices chopped bacon
1/2 cup thinly sliced celery
1 medium finely chopped onion
4 medium cooked and grated potatoes
2 (10 3/4 oz.) cans tomato soup
2 cups water
salt and pepper to taste
2 cups half and half cream

In a skillet, cook bacon pieces, celery and onion until tender, drain. In a sauce pan, add potatoes, bacon mixture, tomato soup, water, salt, and pepper, heat and simmer for 10 minutes. Add cream, heat, but do not boil. Serves 6

# MUSHROOM POTATO SOUP

2 cups chopped mushrooms
1 medium chopped onion
1 cup finely chopped celery
2 Tbs. margarine
3 medium peeled and cubed potatoes
2 tsp. salt
1/8 tsp. pepper
3 cups water
3 Tbs. flour mixed in 1/2 cup water
2 cups light cream or milk
chopped chives

In a large skillet, over medium heat cook mushrooms, onion and celery in margarine until tender. In a large sauce pan, put potatoes, salt, pepper and water, cover and simmer until tender. Add flour and water mixture to potatoes. Add light cream and mushroom mixture, add chives and simmer about 5 minutes. Serves 6.

# CHEESY POTATO SOUP

6 cups chicken broth
6 medium peeled and diced potatoes
1 cup sliced celery
1 grated carrot
1 medium chopped onion
3 Tbs. flour mixed with 1/2 cup water
1 (12 oz.) can evaporated milk
salt and pepper to taste
2 cups grated cheese
2 tsp. parsley flakes

In a large sauce pan, cook first 5 ingredients until tender. Add flour and water mixture to vegetables stirring until thickened. Add milk, salt, pepper, cheese and parsley, heat without boiling. Serves 8.

# CLAM CHOWDER

3/4 cup finely chopped salt pork, or 6 slices chopped bacon
2 (6.5 oz.) cans chopped clams, drained, reserving juice
1/2 cup reserved clam juice
1 1/2 cups water
4 cups diced potatoes
1/2 cup chopped onion
1 1/2 tsp. salt
dash of pepper
1/3 cup pork drippings
2 cups milk
1 (5.12 oz.) can evaporated milk
3 Tbs. flour in 1/2 cup milk

In a skillet, fry pork until crisp. In a sauce pan, put clam juice, water, potatoes, onion, salt, pepper and pork drippings. Cover and cook 20 minutes. Add clams, 2 cups milk and evaporated milk. Blend flour and milk mixture into chowder. Heat to boiling, stirring often. Add pork. Serves 6 to 8.

# CHICKEN CORN CHOWDER

1 (10 3/4 0z.) can cream of potato soup
1 (16 1/2 oz.) can cream style corn
2 tsp. chicken bouillon granules
1 cup diced chicken
2 cups milk
2 Tbs. chopped pimiento

In a large sauce pan stir all ingredients until well blended. Bring to a boil, stirring often. Remove from heat and serve. Serves 4.

# TURKEY POTATO SOUP

4 cups turkey stock
1 cup chopped celery
1 cup chopped onion
1 diced carrot
2 cups diced potatoes
1 cup shredded cabbage
1 Tbs. snipped parsley
1 bay leaf
salt and pepper to taste
2 cups cubed cooked turkey

In a large sauce pan, simmer celery, onions and carrots in stock until partially done. Add potatoes, cabbage, parsley, bay leaf, salt and pepper, simmer until tender. Add turkey. Remove bay leaf before serving. Serves 6 to 8.

# HOME STYLE CLAM CHOWDER

3 (6.5 oz.) cans clams, drained and chopped, reserving juice
4 cups raw cubed potatoes
1 cup diced celery
1 tsp. salt
1/2 cup margarine
3 Tbs. flour in 1/2 cup milk
1/2 cup flour
1 tsp. salt
1/2 tsp. pepper
4 cups milk
1/4 tsp. thyme

In a sauce pan, pour clam juice over vegetables and salt. Add just enough water to cover. Simmer 20 minutes or until vegetables are tender. Combine margarine, milk mixture, flour, salt and pepper in a large sauce pan, add milk. Cook over medium heat, stirring until thickened. Add thyme, cooked vegetables, and clams. Heat and serve. Serves 6.

# QUICK CREAM OF VEGETABLE SOUP

1/4 cup green pepper
1/2 cup medium carrot
1 small onion
1/2 cup of celery, with leaves
1 cup water
2 cups mashed potatoes
3 cups milk
1 cup of half and half cream
2 Tbs. flour mixed with 1/2 cup water
1 Tbs. instant chicken bouillon granules
pepper

In a blender put green pepper, carrot, onion, and celery with 1 cup water. Blend on chop. In a sauce pan, cook over medium heat until tender crisp. Add potatoes, mix well. Add milk and cream. Heat slowly to a boil. Mix flour and water mixture, bouillon and pepper. Add to hot soup. Cook until slightly thickened. May add finely shredded ham, crumbled bacon or snipped parsley. Serves 6.

# BLENDER VEGETABLE SOUP

1 large carrot, cut in chunks
1 chopped rib celery with leaves
1 small onion, halved
1/4 green pepper
1 1/2 cups water
1 bay leaf
2 medium chunked potatoes
4 cups beef broth
2 cups tomato juice
1 Tbs. beef bouillon granules

In a blender put carrot, celery with leaves, onion, green pepper, and water. Blend on chop. Pour into a sauce pan and add bay leaf. Chop potatoes in blender and add to sauce pan. Add beef broth, tomato juice, and beef bouillon granules. Stew until tender. Remove bay leaf before serving. Serves 6.

# SALADS

## GARDEN POTATO SALAD

8 medium potatoes cooked, peeled and cubed
1/2 cup chopped onion
1/4 cup chopped green pepper
1/3 cup thinly sliced radishes
1/2 cup diced cucumber
1/3 cup thinly sliced celery
2 medium tomatoes, seeded and chopped
1 (4.5 oz.) can sliced, ripe olives
4 chopped hard boiled eggs

In a large bowl place all ingredients and gently toss. Add and mix one of the following dressings. Serves 10.

### Blender Mayonnaise

1 tsp. salt
3/4 tsp. dry mustard
1/2 tsp. paprika
dash cayenne
2 egg yolks
2 Tbs. vinegar
2 cups salad oil
2 Tbs. lemon juice

In blender add salt, mustard, paprika, cayenne, egg yolks and vinegar, blend. Slowly drizzle salad oil over rest of ingredients continuously blending. Add lemon juice alternately with last 1/2 cup of oil. Store in refrigerator.

### Bleu Cheese Dressing

Follow blender recipe, add 3/4 cup Bleu cheese, crumbled. Blend until smooth.

Cont'd on page 91

# Italian Cheese Dressing

1 1/2 cups salad oil
2/3 cup vinegar
1/3 cup Parmesan cheese
1 1/2 Tbs. sugar
2 tsp. salt
2 tsp. celery salt
1/8 tsp. pepper
1 tsp. dry mustard
3/4 tsp. oregano
2 cloves crushed garlic
2 tsp. parsley flakes

In blender, combine all ingredients, blend well. Refrigerate until ready to use. Makes about 2 ½ cups.

# Zesty Onion Dressing

2/3 cup salad oil
1/3 cup vinegar
2 tsp. dry mustard
4 tsp. sugar
1 tsp. salt
1 tsp. celery seed
1/3 cup finely minced green onion
2 Tbs. finely chopped green pepper

In blender, add oil, vinegar, dry mustard, sugar, salt and celery seed, blend well. Add onion and green pepper, pour in pint jar and shake well. Makes 1 1/4 cups.

# ITALIAN SWISS POTATO SALAD

4 cups potatoes, cooked, peeled and cubed
3/4 cup chopped celery
3/4 cup finely diced ham
1 cup finely cubed Swiss cheese
1/3 cup minced onion
1/2 cup finely chopped dill pickle
3/4 tsp. salt
dash of pepper
1 cup bottled Italian dressing
1 1/2 Tbs. vinegar
2 tsp. sugar

In a large bowl, mix first 8 ingredients together. In a small bowl mix dressing, vinegar and sugar together. Pour over salad and toss lightly. Serves 8 to 10.

# LUE'S POTATO SALAD

8 medium potatoes, cooked with skins
8 hard boiled eggs
1/2 cup onion
1 cup dill pickle
1/4 cup pickle juice
1 Tbs. mustard
2 1/2 cups mayonnaise

Peel cooled potatoes. In a large bowl, grate potatoes, eggs, onion, and pickle. Sprinkle lightly with salt and pepper. In a small bowl, mix pickle juice and mustard with mayonnaise, add to potato mixture. Serves 8 to 10.

# POTATO TOMATO SALAD

4 medium potatoes, cooked, peeled, cubed
salt and pepper to taste
1 cup peeled and diced cucumber
1 small chopped onion
1 (4.5 oz.) can sliced olives
1/2 cup grated medium Cheddar cheese
1/2 cup chopped green pepper
1/2 cup chopped tomato, drain
1/2 cup bottled Italian dressing
1/2 tsp. ground mustard
1 Tbs. vinegar
8 large tomatoes

In a large bowl toss first 8 ingredients together. In small bowl mix well Italian dressing, mustard, and vinegar, pour over potato mixture and toss. Wash and slice tomato tops off. Scoop center of tomatoes out, leaving a shell, pat dry. Scoop salad into tomato shells, top with sprigs of parsley and chill. Serves 6 to 8.

# POTATO SALAD

8 medium potatoes boiled with skins, cooled, peeled and diced into bowl. Salt lightly and mix.

Add:

1 medium diced onion
3/4 cup chopped dill pickle
8 boiled eggs, peeled and chopped
2 1/2 cups mayonnaise
3 Tbs. pickle juice

In a large bowl, mix all ingredients together, garnish as desired. Chill until served. Serves 8 to 10.

# POTATO PEA SALAD

2 cups potatoes, cooked, peeled and diced
1 cup frozen peas
2 Tbs. chopped onion
2 Tbs. chopped olives
1/2 cup French dressing
1/4 cup mayonnaise

In a bowl, combine potatoes, peas, onions and olives. In a small bowl, mix French dressing and mayonnaise together, toss with potato mixture. Chill before serving. Serves 4.

# MAJESTIC POTATO SALAD

2 envelopes unflavored gelatin
4 cups tomato juice
1 Tbs. lemon juice
1/4 tsp. salt
dash of pepper
6 cups potatoes, cooked, peeled, cooled and cubed
1/4 cup Italian dressing
1 cup salad dressing
1 cup sliced celery
1 cup finely chopped onion
1/2 cup sliced stuffed olives
1/4 cup chopped parsley

In a sauce pan soften gelatin in 1 cup tomato juice over low heat. Add to remaining tomato juice and stir in lemon juice, salt and pepper. Pour into 1 quart ring mold, chill until firm. In a bowl, marinate potatoes in Italian dressing for 1 hour. Add salad dressing, celery, onion and olives, season lightly with salt and pepper. Toss lightly. Unmold aspic on lettuce lined platter. Fill center with potato salad, sprinkle with parsley. Serves 8.

# GERMAN POTATO SALAD

8 slices of bacon
1/2 cup chopped onion
2 Tbs. flour
1 Tbs. sugar
1 1/2 tsp. salt
dash of pepper
1 tsp. celery seed
1/2 cup vinegar
1 cup water
6 cups sliced cooked potatoes
6 hard boiled grated eggs
parsley flakes and pimiento strips

In a skillet, cook bacon until crispy, crumble. Reserve 1/4 cup fat. Cook onion in fat until tender. Add flour. Blend in sugar, salt, pepper, celery seed, vinegar, and water. Cook and stir until thickened. Add bacon, potatoes, and eggs, heat slowly, turning often. Garnish with parsley and pimiento. Serves 8.

# OLD FASHIONED POTATO SALAD

2 Tbs. butter or margarine
2 Tbs. flour
1 cup milk
1/2 cup mayonnaise
3/4 tsp. salt
1/4 tsp. pepper
1 tsp dill
6 medium cooked potatoes peeled, diced and salted lightly
parsley

In a sauce pan, blend and heat butter and flour, add milk and cook until thickened and bubbly. Remove from heat, add mayonnaise, salt, pepper, and dill to milk mixture. Mix into potatoes. Garnish with parsley. Serves 6.

# MARINATED POTATO SALAD

8 medium potatoes, cooked with skins
salt
1 cup chopped celery
6 chopped hard boiled eggs
1/2 cup chopped onion

Cool, peel, and cube potatoes into a large bowl, lightly salt. Add celery, onion, and eggs, chill.

## Dressing

2 tsp. mustard seed
2 tsp. celery seed
1 Tbs. finely chopped red sweet pepper
1 Tbs. finely chopped green pepper
1/2 tsp. pepper
4 Tbs. vinegar
3 cups mayonnaise

In a medium bowl, soak first 5 ingredients in vinegar for several hours. Add mayonnaise and stir into potatoes. Serves 10.

# MUSTARD POTATO SALAD

8 medium cooked and sliced potatoes
1 medium chopped onion
3/4 cup chopped dill pickle
2 ribs chopped celery
1 (4.5 oz.) can chopped ripe olives
8 chopped boiled eggs
2 1/2 cups salad dressing
2 Tbs. prepared mustard
2 to 3 Tbs. pickle juice

In a large bowl, mix first 6 ingredients together. Mix last three ingredients together, add to salad, chill. Garnish with paprika. Serves.10.

# HAM POTATO SALAD

4 cups red, new potatoes, with skins, cut into 1/4-inch slices
boiling water
1 1/2 tsp. salt
1/4 cup oil
2 tsp. sugar
1/2 tsp. salt
1/8 tsp. pepper
1/4 cup thinly sliced green onions
3 Tbs. wine vinegar
1 cup diced ham

In a sauce pan, cover sliced potatoes with water and 1 tsp. salt. Cook until tender, about 10 to 12 minutes. Drain and cool 5 minutes, place in a large bowl. In a small bowl, mix together, oil, sugar, 1/2 tsp. salt, pepper, green onions, and vinegar. Toss with potatoes, cool. Add ham and toss until well mixed. Serves 6.

# HEARTY POTATO SALAD

1 cup chopped onions
1 Tbs. margarine
2/3 cup mayonnaise
1/3 cup red wine vinegar
1 Tbs. sugar
1 1/2 tsp. salt
1/4 tsp. pepper
5 medium cooked potatoes, peeled and sliced
1/4 cup cooked crisp bacon, crumbled
chopped parsley

In a large skillet over medium heat, cook onions in margarine 2 to 3 minutes. Add next 5 ingredients. Add potatoes, continue cooking, stirring constantly. Heat thoroughly but do not boil. Place in a serving dish and garnish with bacon and parsley. Serves 8.

# BLEU CHEESE POTATO TOSS

1/2 cup slivered almonds
5 medium cooked potatoes
1/2 cup celery, sliced
1 (4 oz.) pkg. bleu cheese, crumbled
3 chopped green onions
1 (4.5 oz.) can sliced olives
2 Tbs. snipped parsley
1 cup sour cream
1/3 cup milk
1 Tbs. vinegar
bleu cheese, crumbled

Place almonds in shallow baking pan. Toast at 350° until light brown, cool. Reserve 2 Tbs. for garnish, chop remaining almonds. In a bowl, combine potatoes, celery, cheese, chopped almonds, onions, olives, and parsley. In a small bowl, combine sour cream, milk, and vinegar, add to potato mixture. Toss to mix, chill. Garnish with almonds and bleu cheese. Serves 8.

# MICROWAVE HOT GERMAN POTATO SALAD

1/2 cup chopped onion
4 slices of bacon, cooked crisp and crumbled, reserve drippings
2 Tbs. sugar
1 Tbs. flour
1 tsp. beef bouillon
1 tsp. salt
1/4 tsp. allspice
1/8 tsp. pepper
1/4 cup vinegar
1/2 cup water
4 sliced medium baked potatoes

Cook onions in bacon drippings for 1 minute, uncovered. Stir in sugar, flour, bouillon, salt, allspice and pepper. Blend in vinegar and water. Cook uncovered for 3 minutes, until mixture boils and thickens, stirring twice. Mix in sliced potatoes and place in a serving dish, cover with crumbled bacon. Serves 4 to 6.

# HOT POTATO SALAD

1 cup chopped onion
1 Tbs. butter
1/2 cup mayonnaise
1/3 cup vinegar
1 1/2 tsp. salt
dash of pepper
6 slices of bacon cooked crisp, crumbled
5 medium potatoes, cooked, peeled and sliced

In a large skillet, cook onion and butter over medium heat for 3 minutes. Add mayonnaise, vinegar, salt, pepper, potatoes and bacon, cook, stirring constantly for 2 to 3 minutes, do not boil. Remove from heat, and serve. Serves 6.

# SKILLET POTATO SALAD

1 pkg. (14 oz.) frozen cottage fries
1/2 cup cold water
6 slices bacon, minced
1/2 cup chopped celery
2 Tbs. flour
1 1/2 Tbs. sugar
1 1/2 tsp. salt
1/2 tsp. celery seed
2/3 cup water
1/3 cup vinegar
2 sliced hard cooked eggs
paprika

Place frozen potatoes in cold water in covered skillet, cook over medium heat for 8 to 10 minutes or until tender, drain. Meanwhile, in skillet, cook bacon until softened, add celery and cook until bacon is crisp and celery is golden. Remove from skillet and drain on paper towel. Spoon off excess fat, reserving 2 Tbs. bacon drippings in skillet, blend in flour, sugar, salt and celery seed. Add water and vinegar, cook, stirring until smooth and thickened. Add bacon and celery. Gently fold mixture into hot, well drained potatoes. Turn into 1 1/2 quart bowl, garnish with egg slices and sprinkle with paprika. Serves 4.

# LO-CAL AND LOW SODIUM

## OVEN BAKED FRENCH FRIES

4 medium potatoes, cut in strips, length-wise, about 1/2 inch thick
1 Tbs. oil
1/2 tsp. salt
paprika

Preheat oven to 450°. While cutting potatoes, keep strips in bowl of ice water to crisp. Drain and pat dry on paper towels. Return them to bowl and sprinkle with oil, mix with hands to distribute oil evenly over potatoes. Bake on a cookie sheet until golden brown and tender, about 30 to 40 minutes, turning once. Sprinkle with salt and paprika. Serves 4.

## SPUD AND CELERY FRY
## (LOW SODIUM)

3 large peeled potatoes
2 Tbs. vegetable oil
1/2 cup chopped onion
1/2 tsp. curry powder
1/8 tsp. pepper
1 1/2 cups celery, diagonally sliced
1 tsp. lemon juice

Slice potatoes cross-wise into 1/8 inch slices. Heat oil in large skillet and add potatoes, onion, curry and pepper, toss potatoes in oil to coat evenly. Cover, cook over medium heat for 5 minutes. Uncover, add celery. Cook over medium high heat 15 minutes until potatoes are tender. Sprinkle with lemon juice. Serve immediately. Serves 4.

# BASQUE POTATOES

1 large crushed garlic clove
1 green pepper, cut in thin wedges
2 medium onions, cut in wedges
3 Tbs. olive oil
3 medium tomatoes, cut in wedges
1/3 cup stuffed olives
1 strip orange peel
1/2 tsp. basil
3/4 cup dry white wine
salt and pepper
2 1/2 lbs. potatoes (about 7 medium), boiled or steamed
chopped parsley

In large skillet over medium heat, sauté garlic, green pepper and onions in olive oil, stirring 5 minutes. Add tomatoes, olives, orange peel and basil, stir in wine. Simmer, uncovered, stirring occasionally, 5 minutes more or until vegetables are tender crisp. Remove orange peel. Season to taste with salt and pepper. Mash potatoes, season with salt and pepper. Pile mashed potatoes in shallow serving bowl, spoon vegetables and juices over them. Sprinkle with parsley. 120 calories each. Serves 8.

# VICHYSSOISE

Instant potato flakes or granules for 3 half cup servings
1/3 cup evaporated skim milk
1 (10 3/4 oz.) can of chicken broth
1 tsp. grated onion
1 tsp. chopped chives
1/8 tsp. Tabasco sauce
1 Tbs. lemon juice
1/2 cup plain yogurt
green onions

In a bowl, prepare mashed potatoes as package directs, except substitute water for milk and omit butter. With wire whisk, stir remaining ingredients into mashed potatoes. Add salt to taste. Chill at least 2 hours to serve icy cold. If desired, top with a 1 Tbs. of yogurt and green onion garnish. 110 calories. Serves 3.

# POTATOES O'BRIEN

6 peeled and diced medium potatoes
2 Tbs. cooking oil
1 small finely chopped onion
1 small finely chopped green pepper
2 Tbs. water
1 (4 oz.) can pimientos, drained and cut into strips
salt and pepper

In large bowl, toss diced potatoes in oil to coat evenly. Spread in jelly roll pan. Bake in 400° degree oven for 15 to 20 minutes, or fork tender and lightly golden. Meanwhile, in small, covered heavy sauce pan over low heat, simmer onion and green pepper in water until tender (about 10 minutes). When potatoes are done, add pimiento, onion and green pepper, season with salt and pepper. Toss to mix thoroughly. 135 calories per serving. Serves 6.

# OVEN SCALLOPED POTATOES

6 medium potatoes
1/4 cup finely chopped onion
3 Tbs. flour
1/2 tsp. salt
1/4 tsp. pepper
1 Tbs. margarine
2 1/2 cups skim milk

Preheat oven to 350°. Wash potatoes and cut into thick slices. In a lightly oiled 2 quart casserole, arrange potatoes in 4 layers, sprinkling each of first 3 layers with 1 Tbs. onion, 1 Tbs. flour, 1/8 tsp. salt, and a dash of pepper. Dot each layer with 1 tsp. margarine. Sprinkle top with remaining onion, salt and pepper. Heat milk just to scalding and pour over potatoes. Cover and bake 30 minutes. Uncover and bake 60 to 70 minutes or until potatoes are done. Let stand 5 to 10 minutes before serving. Serves 6.

## LAYERED VEGETABLE CASSEROLE

2 medium sliced potatoes
2 medium sliced carrots
1 large sliced green pepper
2 medium sliced onions
1 (4.5 oz.) can of mushrooms
1 (4.5oz.) small can mild green chili peppers
5 to 6 slices bacon, crisp and crumbled
1 (15 oz.) can tomatoes

In a casserole, layer potatoes, carrots, green pepper, onions, mushrooms and green chili peppers. Add crumbled bacon to tomatoes and pour over vegetables, cover. Bake at 300° for 3 1/2 hours. Serves 4.

# POTATO CASSEROLE

3 medium potatoes, peeled and cubed
water
1 tsp. salt
1/2 cup chopped onion
2 Tbs. butter or margarine
2 Tbs. flour
1 chicken bouillon cube
1 1/4 cups boiling water
1 Tbs. spicy brown mustard
1/4 tsp. pepper
2 Tbs. plain bread crumbs

In a medium sauce pan, combine potatoes with 1 inch cold water and salt. Bring to boil. Cover and reduce heat, simmer 15 to 20 minutes until potatoes are just tender, drain. Place potatoes in a 1 quart casserole and set aside. In a small skillet, sauté onion in butter until tender, stir in flour until smooth, cook 1 minute. Dissolve bouillon cube in boiling water and gradually stir into flour mixture. Cook over low heat, stirring constantly, until sauce thickens. Stir in mustard and pepper, pour sauce over potatoes. Sprinkle with bread crumbs. Bake at 375° for 25 to 30 minutes. 150 calories per serving. Serves 4.

# TWICE BAKED POTATOES, COTTAGE STYLE

6 medium baked potatoes
1 1/2 cups low fat cottage cheese
1 Tbs. chopped chives or green onions
1/2 tsp. salt
paprika and pepper

Carefully scoop out pulp from potato shells. Reserve shells. With fork, mash pulp. Blend in cottage cheese, chives and seasonings. Refill potato shells. Sprinkle with paprika. Reheat in oven 400° for 15 to 20 minutes. 130 calories. If prepared early in day, refrigerate stuffed shells. Reheat at 400° for 30 minutes. Serves 6.

# LEMON BAKED POTATOES

1/3 cup unsalted butter
1 small minced clove garlic
1/8 tsp. hot pepper sauce
1/4 tsp. dried dill
1/8 tsp. lemon rind (opt.)
1 Tbs. lemon juice
3 large potatoes

In a small sauce pan, melt margarine over medium heat. Add garlic, hot pepper sauce, dill, lemon rind and lemon juice, mix well. Cut potatoes in half, length-wise, deeply score cut surfaces being careful not to puncture the skin. Place in a shallow baking pan and brush with butter mixture. Bake in 425° oven for 1 hour, brushing with butter mixture every 15 minutes. Place potatoes under broiler, brush with remaining butter mixture. Broil until golden brown. Serves 6.

# SLIM BAKED POTATOES

4 medium baked potatoes
1/2 cup creamed cottage cheese
1 1/2 tsp. blue cheese
1 1/2 tsp. chopped parsley
1 1/2 tsp. chopped chives
1/4 tsp. salt
1/8 tsp. pepper

While potatoes are baking, place remaining ingredients in container of electric blender. Cover and process until smooth. When potatoes are cooked, remove from oven and cut an x in the top with a fork. Push some of the potato up with slight pressure of the fingers on the side of the potato. Spoon 2 Tbs. topping over each potato. Serves 4.

# BAKED POTATOES OLE

4 baked potatoes
1/2 lb. ground beef
2 Tbs. chopped onion
1/4 cup chopped green pepper
1/4 cup chopped celery
1 Tbs. chili powder
1 (15 oz.) can of tomatoes
1/4 cup water
1/2 tsp. salt
4 cups shredded lettuce
1 cup shredded Mozzarella cheese

While potatoes are baking, cook meat, onion, green pepper, celery and chili powder in a sauce pan over medium heat, cook until vegetables are tender. Add tomatoes, water and salt. Simmer uncovered 20 minutes. When potatoes are cooked, remove from oven and cut an x on top of each potato, push some of potato up with slight pressure of the fingers on the side of the potato. Arrange lettuce on serving platter, place potatoes on lettuce. Spoon meat mixture over each potato and sprinkle with shredded cheese. 290 calories per serving. Serves 4.

# LO-CAL TOPPINGS FOR BAKED POTATOES

1.　　1/2 chopped hard boiled egg, 4 ripe sliced olives, 2 Tbs. chopped green onion. Top with: 1/2 cup low fat plain yogurt mixed with 1/4 tsp. salt and dash of pepper.

2.　　1/2 cup low fat cottage cheese mixed with 2 Tbs. each chopped cucumber, grated carrot and chopped onion. Dash salt and pepper.

3.　　Soft poached egg over 2 Tbs. each chopped tomato, raw or cooked, green pepper, green onion.

# POTATO TUNA SALAD

2 baked potatoes
1 cup cooked green beans
1 cup cooked cauliflower
3/4 cup low calorie bottled Italian salad dressing
3/4 tsp. prepared horseradish
1 tomato, cut into wedges
2 cans (3 1/2 oz.) each water-packed tuna, drained

Slice potatoes 1/4 inch thick, place in a shallow dish. Add green beans and cauliflower. In small bowl or cup, mix together salad dressing and horseradish, pour over vegetables. Refrigerate 4 hours or over night. To serve, arrange vegetables on serving platter with tomato wedges and tuna. 348 calories per serving. Serves 2.

# SKINNY POTATO SALAD

6 medium cooked potatoes, peeled and cubed
1/4 cup sliced cucumber
1/4 cup sliced radishes
2 Tbs. chopped green pepper
1 Tbs. minced onion
1/4 cup sour cream
1/4 cup skim milk
1 Tbs. white wine vinegar
1/8 tsp. Tabasco sauce
salt and pepper to taste
radishes, green pepper and onion.

In a salad bowl mix first 5 ingredients together. Mix sour cream with milk, stir in vinegar, Tabasco, salt and pepper. Pour over salad mixture and mix gently. Chill at least 2 hours. To garnish arrange raw vegetables on top. 80 calories. Serves 8.

# BREAKFAST

## HUNGRY MAN'S BREAKFAST

3/4 lb. ground beef
3/4 lb. ground sausage
3 Tbs. chopped onions
3 Tbs. chopped green pepper
1 pkg. shredded hash browns, thawed
1 1/2 cups shredded Cheddar cheese
1 tsp. salt
1/8 tsp. pepper
6 eggs

In a skillet brown ground beef, sausage, onion and green pepper, remove from skillet. In same skillet, brown hash browns in 3 Tbs. meat drippings. Mix ground beef mixture, hash browns, cheese, salt and pepper, turn into 8 x 10 unbuttered baking dish. Make 6 indentations in mixture, carefully break 1 egg into each indentation. Bake uncovered, at 350° for 20 to 25 minutes. Cut into 6 portions.

## IDAHO FARMERS BREAKFAST

1/3 cup chopped onion
1/4 cup chopped green pepper
1/4 cup butter
1 cup ham cut in thin strips
2 medium potatoes, cooked, peeled and cubed
3/4 tsp. salt
6 beaten eggs
2 Tbs. water
1/2 tsp. salt
dash of pepper

Cook onion and green pepper in butter until crisp and tender. Add ham, potatoes and salt, cook over medium heat for 10 minutes, stirring occasionally. Combine eggs, water, 1/2 tsp. salt, and pepper. Pour over potato mixture. Cook over low heat. until eggs are set. Serves 6.

# CANADIAN HASH BROWN BREAKFAST

1/3 cup chopped onion
1 Tbs. parsley flakes
3 cups hash browns
3 Tbs. butter
3 Tbs. flour
3/4 tsp. salt
1/8 tsp. pepper
3/4 cup milk
1/2 cup sour cream
8 slices Canadian bacon
4 eggs

Mix onion and parsley with hash browns in a buttered 9-inch square baking dish. Melt butter in saucepan, blend in flour, salt and pepper. Add milk, cook over low heat, stirring constantly, until thickened. Remove from heat, blend in sour cream. Pour over hash browns, lifting hash browns with fork to allow sauce to mix in. Arrange bacon in an overlapping row down center of dish. Bake at 350° for 45 minutes, remove from oven. Make 2 indentations on each side of bacon, place 1 egg in each indentation. Season with salt and pepper. Bake 15 to 20 minutes longer or until eggs are set. Serves 4.

# POTATO HOT CAKES

2 cups flour
2/3 cup potato flakes
3 tsp. baking powder
1 tsp. salt
1 Tbs. sugar
1/2 tsp. cream of tartar
1/2 cup, plus 1 Tbs. oil
2 1/2 cups milk
2 eggs, slightly beaten

In a bowl, mix flour, potato flakes, baking powder, salt, sugar and cream of tarter together. Add milk and oil, blend. Stir in beaten eggs. Bake on hot griddle until golden brown on both sides.

# HASH AND EGGS

4 cups hash browns
2 Tbs. butter
1 (10 3/4 oz.) can cream of celery soup
1/3 cup milk
1 tsp. ground mustard
1/8 tsp. pepper
1 (15 oz.) can of corned beef hash
4 eggs

In a skillet, cook hash browns in hot butter for 2 minutes stirring often. Add next 4 ingredients, heat thoroughly. Stir in corned beef, reduce the heat to low. Make 4 indentations in hash brown mixture break an egg into each. Sprinkle eggs lightly with salt. Cover and cook 10 minutes or until egg whites are set. Serves 4.

# HEN NESTS

1 (32 oz.) pkg. hash brown potatoes
butter
4 eggs
salt
pepper

Stir and brown hash browns on hot buttered griddle. Shape into four nests. Break 1 egg into each nest. Sprinkle with salt and pepper, cover. Cook until egg whites are set. Serve immediately. Serves 4.

# BREAKFAST IN A POTATO NEST

## Crust

3 cups shredded hash browns
1/2 cup grated Parmesan cheese
1/2 tsp. salt
1 egg

In a bowl, mix all ingredients together and line 9-inch pie plate to form crust.

## Filling

1 1/2 cups of cooked sausage
6 eggs, well beaten
3/4 cup milk
1 Tbs. grated onion
1/2 tsp. salt
3/4 tsp. Italian seasoning
3/4 cup shredded Cheddar cheese

In a bowl, mix all ingredients together and pour into shell. Bake at 375° for 35 to 40 minutes or until knife inserted in center comes out clean. Let stand 5 minutes before serving. Serves 4.

# POTATO OMELET

1/3 cup chopped green pepper
1/3 cup chopped green onion
3 cups shredded hash browns
3/4 tsp. salt
6 eggs
3/4 tsp. salt
Dash of pepper
1/3 cup milk
1 1/2 cup grated sharp American cheese
1 cup shredded ham or crumbled crispy bacon

In a skillet, cook green pepper and onion in 3 Tbs. bacon drippings or butter. Add salted hash browns to green pepper and onion mixture, stir, and brown on one side. In a bowl, blend eggs, salt, pepper and milk. Pour over potatoes. Top with sharp American cheese and ham. Cook over low heat. When egg is set, fold in half. May garnish with salsa sauce or parsley. Serves 4.

# POTATO WAFFLES

2 cups flour
1 cup potato flakes
1 1/2 Tbs. sugar
3 tsp. baking powder
1/2 tsp. cream of tartar
1 tsp. salt
3 egg yolks
2 3/4 cups milk
2/3 cup salad oil
3 egg whites, stiffly beaten

In a bowl, mix dry ingredients together, add egg yolks, milk and oil, mix well. Fold in beaten egg whites. Bake in waffle iron according to directions.

# BREAKFAST PIES

5 slices bacon, cooked crisp and crumbled
4 cups shredded hash browns
1 Tbs. grated onion
2 Tbs. milk
3 eggs, beaten
1 tsp. celery salt
dash of pepper
dash Tabasco sauce
2 pkgs. (10 each) refrigerated biscuits
1 1/2 cups grated Cheddar cheese

Cook and crumble bacon. Brown hash browns and onion in 3 Tbs. bacon drippings. Add milk to beaten eggs. Mix eggs, celery salt, pepper, and Tabasco sauce with potatoes. Flatten 10 biscuits with rolling pin. Place on baking sheet. Divide the filling onto each biscuit, sprinkle cheese over each pie. Flatten remaining biscuits and place over pie tops, moisten edges and crimp to seal. With a fork pierce tops once. Bake 375° for 15 to 20 minutes or until golden brown. Makes 10 pies.

# POTATO PANCAKES

6 medium potatoes, peeled and grated
1 small grated onion
2 Tbs. flour
5 strips bacon, crispy cooked, crumbled
2 eggs, beaten
1 1/2 tsp. salt
dash of pepper
3 Tbs. butter

In a bowl, mix first 7 ingredients together. Heat butter in skillet. Do not let butter get brown. Pour 1/3 cup of batter for each pancake. Flatten and turn when browned. Fry until crispy brown, remove to paper towels. Keep hot. Serve with honey and butter, favorite syrup, or may be eaten plain.

# SAUSAGE HASH BROWN OMELET

1/2 lb. bulk pork sausage
2 cups cooked shredded potatoes
1/4 cup butter
1/4 cup chopped green pepper
1/4 cup chopped onion
6 eggs
1/4 cup milk
salt
dash of pepper
3/4 cup shredded processed American cheese

Cook sausage, drain. Melt butter in skillet, combine potato, green pepper and onion, press into skillet. Season with salt and pepper. Cook over low heat until underside is crisp and brown. Blend eggs, milk, salt, and dash of pepper, pour over potatoes, top with cheese and sausage. Cover, cook over low heat for 6 to 8 minutes. Loosen omelet, cut into wedges and serve. 1 cup ham or crumbled cooked bacon may be used instead of sausage. Serves 4.

# BREAKFAST BURRITOS

12 (10 inch) flour tortillas
24 sausage links
1/4 cup butter or margarine
1 (24 oz.) pkg. of shredded hash browns
8 large eggs, beaten
1 1/2 cups grated Cheddar cheese
1 (4 oz.) can green chilies, drained and chopped
1 (8 oz.) bottle salsa sauce
1 cup chopped onion

Heat oven on warm. Wrap tortillas in foil and put in oven to keep warm. Brown sausage links. Remove and keep warm. Melt butter in skillet, add hash browns. Cook until browned, reduce heat to medium, add eggs, cook 3 to 5 minutes, stirring constantly, until eggs are set. Unwrap tortillas, top each with potato mixture. Sprinkle with cheese, chilies, sauce, onion, and 2 sausage links. Roll up tortillas.

# SAUSAGE POTATO POCKETS

3/4 lbs. bulk Italian sausage
1 clove minced garlic
1/4 cup chopped onion
1 1/2 cups frozen hash browns
1 egg, slightly beaten
1 cup grated cheese
3 Tbs. grated Parmesan cheese
2 (8 oz.) cans refrigerated crescent dinner rolls

### Egg Wash

1 egg, slightly beaten
1 Tbs. water

In a skillet brown sausage, garlic and onion, drain well. In a small skillet brown hash browns with 2 Tbs. butter. Add sausage mixture to the potatoes, add beaten egg and cheeses, mix well. Separate dough into 8 rectangles. Press perforations to seal, flatten slightly. Spoon about 1/2 cup mixture on half of each rectangle to within 1/2 inch of edges of dough. Bring unfilled half of dough over filling and pinch edges to seal. Place on cookie sheet, brush with egg and water wash. Bake at 350° until golden brown 20 to 25 minutes. Makes 8 pockets.

# MASHED POTATO PANCAKES

2 cups mashed potatoes
4 eggs
1 pkg. onion soup mix
1/2 cup milk
butter

In a bowl, mix potatoes, eggs, soup and milk, mix together. Fry on hot, buttered griddle until golden brown on both sides.

# APPETIZERS

## FRENCH FRIES

Cut peeled potatoes length-wise in strips. Soak in cold water 1 hour. Drain on paper towels. Fry small amount of potatoes at a time in deep hot oil, 360° F, until light brown. Drain, sprinkle with salt. Serve hot.

## POTATO WEDGES

6 to 8 small potatoes cooked and cooled with skins on
2 eggs
2 Tbs. flour
1/2 tsp. salt
1/2 cup water
2 cups crushed cornflakes
1/2 cup flour

Peel and cut potatoes into 4 to 6 wedges each. Salt lightly. In a bowl, beat eggs with flour, salt, and water. Dip potatoes in egg mixture, then cornflake mixture. Deep fry at 360° until golden brown. Drain on paper towel. Plain potato wedges may be deep fried without dip and crumb mixture. Sprinkle with onion salt, chili powder, taco mix or Parmesan cheese.

## POTATO WHEELS

Wash and peel 5 or 6 medium potatoes. Slice potatoes into rounds 1/4 inch thick. Soak in cold water for 1 hour. Place on paper towels to take up excess moisture. Deep fry at 360°. Drain on paper towels, sprinkle with salt. May sprinkle with grated Parmesan cheese, chili powder or onion salt. Also, may use cooked potatoes with or without skins in place of raw potatoes.

# POTATO CHIPS

Wash and peel potatoes. Use a potato peeler or vegetable slicer to slice into thin slices, lengthwise. Soak in cold water for about 1 hour, changing the water twice. Drain on paper toweling. Heat oil to 360° in a deep fat fryer or deep skillet. Drop the slices separately into hot oil. Shake the basket or use a slotted spoon to keep potato chips separated. Remove chips as they become golden brown. Drain on paper towel and salt lightly.

# POTATO CHIP SNACKS

7 to 8 cups crinkle cut potato chips
1 cup shredded processed American cheese
Schilling vegetable seasoning

Spread potato chips on a baking sheet. Sprinkle with cheese. Sprinkle vegetable seasoning as desired. Heat at 350° for 5 minutes or until cheese melts. Serve hot.

# CRISPY POTATO SKINS

4 large baking potatoes
4 Tbs. melted butter
salt and pepper to taste

Bake potatoes in the usual way. When done, cool slightly, then cut into wedge shaped quarters. Scoop out almost all the pulp and use for hash browns or other dishes. Place wedges, skin side down, on a baking sheet. Brush with melted butter and sprinkle with salt and pepper. Bake at 425° for 10 minutes or until crispy. Makes 16 wedges.

### Other Toppings

Grated cheese, Parmesan cheese, pizza sauce, cheese, melted butter, chili powder and toasted sesame seeds.

# BAKED CRUNCHY POTATOES

1/3 cup margarine
4 large potatoes, sliced 1/2 inch thick

Melt margarine on a large cookie sheet. Add potatoes, single layer, turn to butter both sides.

## Topping

1 cup crushed cornflakes or crushed rice krispies
2 tsp. salt
2 cups shredded Cheddar cheese
2 tsp. onion powder
2 tsp. paprika

Sprinkle over potatoes. Bake at 375° for 30 minutes or until done and crispy. Serve immediately.

# POTATO PUFFS

4 cups mashed potatoes
2 egg yolks, slightly beaten
1 Tbs. minced onion
1/4 cup flour, sifted
1 tsp. baking powder
1 tsp. salt
2 egg whites, stiffly beaten

In a bowl, combine potatoes with egg yolks and onion. In a small bowl, sift together flour, baking powder, and salt. Add to potatoes, mix well. Fold in stiff-beaten egg whites. Drop by rounded Tbs. into hot oil. Cook until puffs are brown, turning once. Drain on paper towel. Serve hot.

# NACHO ROUNDS

1 large potato, wash but do not peel
2 Tbs. hot taco sauce
1 (4 oz.) can mild or hot chilies, drained and chopped
3/4 cup shredded sharp Cheddar cheese

Preheat oven to 350°. Cut potato crosswise into 20 slices. Place in single layer on a buttered baking sheet. Brush potato slices with taco sauce, sprinkle with chilies and cheese. Bake 25 minutes or until potatoes are tender and cheese is golden brown. Serve warm. May use toppings listed with the microwave nacho rounds.

# MICROWAVE NACHO ROUNDS

To prepare in a microwave oven, prepare potatoes as directed above. Place half of potato slices in circle on micro-proof plate. Cook on high 6 to 8 minutes or until potatoes are tender. Repeat with remaining slices. Let stand 3 minutes before serving.

### Toppings

For Italian flavor, use pizza sauce or tomato sauce with Italian seasonings, chopped onions, and cheese in place of taco sauce, chilies and Cheddar cheese.

# POTATO BALLS

3 cups mashed potatoes
2 Tbs. grated onion
1 tsp. salt
2 eggs
2/3 cup flour
1 tsp. baking powder
crushed rice krispies or cornflakes

In a bowl, mix first 6 ingredients well. Form into balls. Roll in crushed rice krispies or cornflakes. Deep fry in hot oil, 360° until golden brown. Drain on paper towels.

# POTATO BURGERS

1/2 lb. ground beef
1 medium potato, peeled, grated and drained
1 small grated onion
any of the following herbs to taste, garlic, sage, oregano, thyme, chili powder, curry powder, marjoram, cumin, or basil.

In a bowl, combine ingredients and shape into burgers or small appetizer sized balls. Fry 6 to 8 minutes on each side or until done.

# SMORGASBORD BALLS

2 lbs. ground beef
1 lb. bulk sausage
3/4 cup grated raw potato
3 Tbs. grated onion
1/2 tsp. allspice
1 1/2 tsp. salt
1/2 tsp. pepper

In a bowl, mix all ingredients and shape into small walnut sized balls. Bake for 15 to 20 minutes in a shallow pan at 350°. Serve hot with toothpicks for handles.

# SPICY MEATBALLS

2 lbs. ground steak
1 lb. ground pork
2 eggs, well beaten
1 cup mashed potatoes
1 cup dried bread crumbs
1 tsp. brown sugar
2 tsp. salt
1/8 tsp. pepper
1/2 tsp. ginger
1/2 tsp. cloves
1/2 tsp. nutmeg
1/2 tsp. allspice
2 cups cream

In a bowl, combine all ingredients except cream. Mix well, form into balls. Roll in flour and brown in small amount hot fat. Add cream, cover, simmer slowly until meat is tender.

# POTATO STUFFED HAM ROLLUPS

1 large potato cooked with skin, cooled, peeled, and grated
2 Tbs. grated onion
2 Tbs. grated dill pickle
2 Tbs. finely chopped celery
3/4 cup shredded Cheddar cheese
3/4 cup sour cream
12 to 15 ham slices

In a bowl, mix first 6 ingredients together. Spoon mixture on one end of ham slice, roll up and cut in two. Secure with party picks if needed. Chill for several hours or over night. This enhances the flavor.

# PO PIZZA SQUARES

8 hash brown patties
8 Tbs. pizza sauce
1 lb. cooked sausage, crumbled
2 Tbs. minced onion
1 (4.5 oz.) can sliced olives
1 (4.5 oz.) can chopped mushrooms
1 cup grated Mozzarella cheese
1 cup grated sharp Cheddar cheese
butter

On a well buttered grill or in a heavy skillet, brown hash brown patties on both sides. Spread each with 1 Tbs. pizza sauce. Divide cooked sausage, onion, olives and mushrooms to top each patty. Sprinkle each with grated mixed cheese. Place on cookie sheet and bake until cheese melts, 400° for 5 to 7 minutes. Makes 8 squares.

# SPICY POTATO ONION FRITTERS

2 Tbs. chopped mild chili peppers
2 cups mashed potatoes, no milk
1 small finely chopped onion
1 pkg. ranch dressing
1 egg
1 cup flour
1/2 tsp. salt
1/2 tsp. cream of tartar
3/4 tsp. baking powder
1 cup water
1 egg

Mix first 5 ingredients together. Form into 1 inch balls. Mix flour, salt, cream of tartar, baking powder, water and egg together. Dip balls into batter, deep fry in hot oil, drain on paper towel.

# POTATO GUACAMOLE

1 (2/3 cup) avocado peeled, pitted and mashed
1 1/2 Tbs. lemon juice
1 cup potatoes, seasoned and mashed
1/4 cup canned diced green chilies
1/4 cup canned chopped tomato
2 Tbs. chopped green onion
1 clove garlic, crushed

In a bowl blend avocado and lemon juice, mix in remaining ingredients. Cover and chill 1 hour. Serve as a dip with raw vegetable chunks or potato chips, or use with Mexican foods. Makes 2 1/4 cups.

# POTATO DIP

3 medium potatoes, peeled and cooked until tender
1 cup buttermilk
1 tsp. horseradish
1/2 cup sour cream

In a blender put potatoes and buttermilk, blend until smooth. Add horseradish and sour cream, mix. Refrigerate over night. Serve with crackers or fresh vegetables. Makes 2 1/2 cups.

# SWEET POTATOES

## BOILED SWEET POTATOES

Scrub and cut off dried ends. In a deep saucepan, cover sweet potatoes, in skins, with water. Cover and cook for 35 minutes or until tender. Drain and peel off skins. Serve with butter, brown sugar and butter or cooked crisp bacon.

## BAKED SWEET POTATOES

Scrub and cut off dried ends. Dry and rub with vegetable oil. Bake at 350° for 50 to 60 minutes. Cover or wrap in foil to keep hot. Serve with butter, brown sugar and butter or applesauce and crumbled bacon.

## FRENCH FRIED SWEET POTATOES

Scrub and peel 3 medium sweet potatoes. Slice potatoes into 1/2-inch sticks. Soak in ice water for 2 hours. Remove to paper towels to dry. Fry in deep hot fat, 360° until browned, 3 to 5 minutes, drain, sprinkle with salt. Serve with applesauce or honey and butter dip.

## FRIED SWEET POTATOES

6 cups sweet potatoes, peeled and sliced thin
6 to 8 bacon slices, diced
salt and pepper to taste

In a skillet, sauté bacon until edges start to curl, add sliced sweet potatoes, salt and pepper. Cover and cook over medium heat for 3 to 5 minutes. Remove lid and turn potatoes. Continue to cook until tender, turning occasionally. Serves 6 to 8.

# YAM AND SAUSAGE SKILLET

1 (8 oz.) pkg. sausage links
1 (3 oz.) pkg. orange flavored gelatin
1 (20 oz.) can pineapple chunks, drained, reserve juice
1/3 cup packed brown sugar
3 Tbs. butter
1 Tbs. minced onion
2 tsp. dry mustard
1/4 cup lemon juice
1/2 tsp. salt
1 (20 oz.) can yams, drained
snipped parsley

In a large skillet, brown sausage links. Remove sausage. In the same skillet, combine gelatin with 1/2 cup pineapple juice, add next 6 ingredients. Heat, stirring constantly until mixture boils. Add yams and pineapple, reduce heat and simmer for 15 minutes, stirring often. Add sausage, continue to cook, basting often, for 5 minutes. Sprinkle with parsley. Serves 8.

# SWEET POTATO CASSEROLE

3 lbs. sweet potatoes
2 eggs
1/2 cup packed brown sugar
1/2 cup melted butter
1 tsp. salt
2 tsp. cinnamon
orange juice
1/3 cup chopped pecans

Peel, dice and cook sweet potatoes. Drain and mash. In a bowl, beat together potatoes, eggs, 1/4 cup brown sugar, 1/4 cup melted butter, salt, cinnamon and orange juice (enough to moisten), pour into a casserole. Top with pecans, 1/4 cup butter and 1/4 cup brown sugar. Bake at 375° for 25 minutes. Serves 8.

# APPLE CINNAMON SWEET POTATO

1 (16 oz.) can sweet potatoes, cut in 1-inch slices
2 cups applesauce
3 Tbs. red cinnamon candies
1 Tbs. flour
1/2 cup packed brown sugar
3 Tbs. butter
1/2 tsp. salt

Layer half the sweet potatoes in a buttered casserole dish. Heat apple sauce and candies together until candies are melted. Pour half of applesauce over potatoes. Repeat with layers of remaining sweet potato and applesauce. Combine flour, sugar, butter and salt, crumble over top. Bake covered at 350° for 50 minutes. Serves 8.

# MAPLE SWEET POTATOES

6 medium cooked sweet potatoes
2/3 cup maple syrup
2 Tbs. butter
1 tsp. salt
1/2 cup apple juice

Peel and slice sweet potatoes into a casserole dish. Heat remaining ingredients to boiling, pour over potatoes and bake at 350° for 45 minutes. Serves 8.

# ORANGE SWEET POTATOES

8 medium cooked and sliced sweet potatoes
1/2 cup sugar
1/2 cup packed brown sugar
1/4 cup undiluted frozen orange juice
1 Tbs. cornstarch
1/3 cup butter

Place sliced sweet potatoes in a baking dish. Cook sugars, juice, and cornstarch, bring to a boil and cook 1 minute. Add butter, pour mixture over potatoes. Bake at 350° for 30 minutes. Serves 8.

# SWEET POTATO PUFF

2 cups cooked sweet potatoes, peeled and mashed
1/2 cup milk
2 Tbs. butter
1/2 tsp. salt
1/8 tsp. allspice
2 egg yolks
2 egg whites

Combine potatoes, milk, butter, salt and allspice in a large mixing bowl. Beat with electric mixer until fluffy. Add egg yolks, beat well. Beat egg whites until stiff, carefully fold into potato mixture. Turn into ungreased 1-quart casserole dish. Bake at 350° for 1 hour or until heated through. Serve with butter. Serves 4.

# SWEET POTATO BOATS

3 large sweet potatoes
1/2 cup cranberry relish
1 tsp. grated orange peel
1/2 cup raisins or currants
1/2 cup packed brown sugar
1/3 tsp. salt
3 Tbs. butter
1/3 cup chopped walnuts

In a saucepan, cook sweet potatoes in salted water just until tender. Cut in half, length-wise. Scoop out center of sweet potato halves. In a bowl, combine sweet potato centers, cranberry relish, and orange peel, beat until fluffy. Stir in raisins and scoop potato mixture into potato halves. Combine brown sugar and salt, cut in butter and stir in walnuts. Sprinkle over tops of sweet potatoes. Bake at 350° for 30 minutes. Serves 6.

# HAM SWEET POTATO ROLL

1/2 lb. ground beef
3/4 lb. ground ham
3/4 cup crushed cracker crumbs
1 large egg
3/4 cup milk
1/2 tsp. salt
1/8 tsp. pepper
2 cups mashed sweet potatoes
1/4 cup packed brown sugar
3/4 tsp. salt

In a bowl, mix first 7 ingredients and spread on wax paper into a rectangle 1/2 inch thick. In a bowl, mix sweet potatoes, brown sugar and salt, spread over meat mixture. Form into a roll and put into a greased baking dish. Bake 1 hour and 15 minutes at 350°. Serves 6 to 8.

# SWEET POTATO CROQUETTES

2 cups cooked mashed sweet potato
1 tsp. salt
dash of pepper
1 1/2 Tbs. brown sugar
2 Tbs. melted butter
12 marshmallows
butter, melted
2/3 cup crushed fine cornflakes

In a bowl, mix first 5 ingredients. Shape mixture into balls around marshmallows. Roll in melted butter, then in cornflake crumbs. Bake in a shallow baking pan at 350° for 12 minutes longer. Makes 12 croquettes.

# SWEET POTATO WAFFLES

4 Tbs. butter
1 Tbs. sugar
1 egg, separated
1 cup mashed sweet potatoes
3/4 cup flour
2 tsp. baking powder
1/4 tsp. cream of tartar
1/4 tsp. salt
1/4 tsp. nutmeg
1 cup milk

In a mixing bowl cream butter and sugar, add egg yolk and sweet potatoes. Mix together flour, baking powder, cream of tartar, salt and nutmeg, alternately add milk and flour mixture to sweet potatoes. Beat egg white until stiff, fold into batter. Bake in heated waffle iron until golden brown. Serve with powdered sugar and cinnamon or with maple syrup and butter.

# SWEET POTATO PIE

1 1/4 cup mashed sweet potato
1/2 cup packed brown sugar
1/4 tsp. salt
1 tsp. cinnamon
1/4 tsp. allspice
1 tsp. vanilla
2 eggs
1 Tbs. cornstarch
1 (5.12 oz.) can evaporated milk

In a bowl, whip sweet potatoes, removing all the stringy fiber. Add all ingredients except milk. Beat well with an electric mixer. Reduce speed, gradually add milk. Pour into unbaked pie crust and bake at 350º for 35 to 40 minutes or until set. Serve with whipped cream and sliced almonds. Serves 6.

# BREADS

## POTATO BREAD

9 to 10 cups flour
1/4 cup sugar
2 pkgs. active dry yeast
1 Tbs. salt
4 cups hot milk, about 125°
1 egg
1 cup mashed potatoes

In a large bowl with an electric mixer, mix 3 cups of flour, sugar, yeast and salt. Gradually add hot milk, beating 2 minutes on medium speed, scraping bowl often with rubber spatula. Add egg, potatoes and 2 cups of flour, beat on high speed for 2 minutes, scraping bowl occasionally. Stir in 3 to 4 cups flour or enough to make a stiff dough. Turn out dough on to a floured surface and knead 8 to 10 minutes until smooth and elastic. Shape into ball and place in a greased bowl. Grease the surface, cover with damp cloth and let rise in warm place until doubled, about 45 minutes. Divide dough into 4 equal pieces, shape each into a loaf. Place into greased pans, cover and let rise about 1 hour, or until dough has risen just above the rim of the pans. Bake at 400° for about 45 minutes or until sounds hollow when tapped. Brush tops of loaves with butter or oil, remove from pans and cool on racks. 4 loaves.

# WHOLE WHEAT POTATO BREAD

1 pkg. active dry yeast
2 tsp. sugar
1/2 cup warm water
2 cups scalded milk
2 cups mashed potatoes
1/4 cup shortening
1 tsp. salt
1 Tbs. caraway seed
4 cups whole-wheat flour
4 cups white flour

In a small bowl, sprinkle yeast and sugar in warm water, stir until dissolved. In mixing bowl, combine milk, mashed potatoes, shortening, salt and caraway seeds. Add 1 cup each whole wheat and white flour. Beat until smooth. Cool to lukewarm, stir in yeast, add enough remaining flour to make stiff dough. Turn on a lightly floured surface and knead 10 minutes or until dough is smooth and elastic. Place in buttered bowl, turning to butter top, cover. Let rise until doubled in bulk. Punch down and turn on to lightly floured surface. Knead dough an additional 5 minutes. Divide into 2 equal portions and form into round loaves. Butter two 8-inch pie or cake pans. May use standard greased loaf pans. Place loaves in pans, cover and let rise until doubled. Brush loaves with water and slit tops with sharp knife. Bake at 400° for 30 minutes or until loaves sound hollow. Makes 2 round loaves.

# OLD FASHIONED POTATO LOAVES

2 medium potatoes, peeled and diced
water
hot tap water
2 pkgs. active dry yeast
2 Tbs. soft margarine or butter
2 Tbs. sugar
1 tsp. salt
1 cup warm milk
6 1/2 to 7 1/2 cups unsifted flour

In a saucepan, cover potatoes with water and cook until tender, drain, reserving liquid. Add hot tap water to potato water to make 1 cup, cool to warm. Mash potatoes, set aside. Pour warm potato water into a large warm bowl. Sprinkle in yeast, stir until dissolved. Add margarine, sugar and salt. Stir in mashed potatoes, warm milk and 3 cups of flour, beat until smooth. Stir in enough additional flour to make a stiff dough. Turn out onto a lightly floured board, knead until smooth and elastic, about 8 to 10 minutes. Place in greased bowl, turning to grease top, cover. Let rise in warm place, free from draft, until doubled, about 35 minutes, punch dough down, turn over in bowl, cover and let rise again about 20 minutes. Punch dough down. Turn out onto lightly floured board, divide in half. Roll each half into 14 x 9 inch rectangle. Shape into loaves. Place in 2 greased 9 x 5 x 3 inch loaf pans, cover. Let rise in warm place, free from draft, until doubled for about 50 minutes. Dust loaves with flour. Bake at 375° for 35 to 40 minutes or until done. Remove from pans and cool on wire racks. Add 1 cup chopped fresh onions and/or 1 Tbs. dill seed. Makes 2 loaves.

# POTATO ORANGE NUT BREAD

3/4 cup sugar
2 Tbs. shortening
1 egg
3/4 cup cooked grated potatoes
1 cup orange juice
1/4 cup water
4 tsp. grated orange peel
1/3 cup dry powdered milk
3 cups flour
3 1/2 tsp. baking powder
1/2 tsp. salt
3/4 cup chopped walnuts

In a mixing bowl, mix sugar, shortening, egg and potatoes thoroughly. Stir in orange juice, water, and orange peel. In a bowl, combine dry ingredients, stir into potato mixture. Add walnuts,. Pour into greased large loaf pan. Bake 350° for 60 to 70 minutes, or until tooth pick stuck in center comes out clean.. Makes 1 large loaf.

# POTATO CINNAMON NUT BREAD

3/4 cup sugar
2 Tbs. soft shortening
1 egg
3/4 cup cooked grated potatoes
1 1/4 cups water or potato water
2/3 cup dry powdered milk
3 cups flour
3 tsp. baking powder
1/2 tsp. salt
2 tsp. cinnamon
3/4 cup chopped walnuts
3/4 cups raisins, plumped in warm water and drained

Mix sugar, shortening, egg and potatoes thoroughly. Stir in water. Combine dry ingredients, mix in. Add in walnuts and raisins. Pour into greased loaf pan. Bake at 350° for 60 to 70 minutes. 1 loaf.

# SPUD AND CHEESE SPOON ROLLS

3 to 3 1/4 cups flour
1 Tbs. sugar
2 tsp. salt
1 pkg. active dry yeast
2/3 cup potato flakes
1 cup boiling water
3/4 cup evaporated milk
1/4 cup shortening
1 egg
1 cup shredded cheese

    In a large bowl combine 2 cups flour, sugar, salt, yeast, and potato flakes. In a bowl, combine boiling water, milk and shortening, cool to lukewarm. Add egg and warm liquid to flour mixture. Using a mixer, blend at low speed until dampened, beat 3 minutes at medium speed. Stir in remaining flour and cheese to form a stiff batter, cover. Let rise in warm place until light and doubled in size, about 1 1/2 hours. Stir down batter. Spoon batter into 24 well greased muffin cups, cover. Let rise until doubled, 50 to 60 minutes. Bake at 375° for 20 to 25 minutes or until golden brown. Remove from pan immediately. Makes 24 rolls.

# POTATO BUTTERHORNS

2 Tbs. sugar
1 Tbs. salt
1/4 cup shortening
2 cups hot mashed potatoes
2 eggs, beaten
1 pkg. active dry yeast
2 cups milk
6 cups flour
egg wash, 1 egg white beaten with 1 Tbs. water

In a bowl, mix sugar, salt, shortening and potatoes, cool. Add eggs. Soften yeast in milk, add to potato mixture. Add flour, a small amount at a time, beating well after each addition. Turn out onto lightly floured surface, knead until smooth and elastic, about 8 minutes. Dough should be as soft as possible to handle. Place in greased bowl, turning once, cover with damp cloth. Set in warm place, let rise until doubled. Divide dough into 4 parts. Turn each part onto lightly floured surface, roll into a circle 1/2 inch thick. Cut into wedges, having each outer edge 3 inches wide. Begin on outside edge and roll toward the center. Form into crescents. Place on greased baking sheets and brush with egg wash. Cover with damp cloth and let rise until doubled in bulk. Bake at 450° for 12 minutes or until golden brown.

# NO KNEAD POTATO ROLLS

1 cup mashed potatoes
1/3 cup sugar
3/4 cup shortening
1 tsp. salt
1 cup scalded milk
2 eggs
1 pkg. active dry yeast dissolved in 3 Tbs. lukewarm water
5 cups flour

In a bowl, mix potato, sugar, shortening and salt. Add milk and eggs. When lukewarm, add yeast and 1 cup of flour. Beat well, let rise 2 hours in warm place. Stir in 4 cups flour and let rise 2 hours longer. Make into rolls, using as little flour as possible. Let rise 1 hour or until double. Bake 15 to 18 minutes at 375°. Makes 3 to 3 1/2 dozen.

# POTATO ROLLS

1 pkg. active dry yeast
1/4 cup lukewarm water
1 egg, beaten
3 Tbs. milk
1/3 cup melted shortening
2 Tbs. sugar or honey
1/2 cup lukewarm, cooked and sieved potatoes
1 1/2 tsp. salt
3 cups flour
melted butter

In a bowl, add yeast to water and stir until dissolved, add beaten egg. In a large bowl, combine milk, shortening, honey, potatoes and salt. Add egg and yeast to the potato mixture. Add flour, mixing to make a soft, but not sticky dough. Knead on lightly floured board until surface of dough is smooth and small blisters appear just under the surface, about 7 minutes. Place in greased bowl and cover. Let rise until double, about 1 1/2 hours. Shape into rolls, place in greased pans, and let rise until double in size. Bake 400° 15 to 20 minutes. Butter tops. Makes 2 to 3 dozen.

# POTATO BUTTERMILK ROLLS

3/4 cup hot mashed potato
1/3 cup butter
2 cups buttermilk
1 pkg. active dry yeast
2 Tbs. sugar
1 Tbs. salt
2 eggs
7 1/2 cups flour

In a large mixing bowl, mix together potato and butter. In a saucepan, heat buttermilk to lukewarm. Measure 1/2 cup of buttermilk with yeast, sugar and salt. Let sit 10 minutes. Add remaining buttermilk and mix with potato. Beat until light, add eggs. Sift before measuring 7 1/2 cups flour. Stir in 6 cups flour. Knead in remaining flour. Place dough in greased bowl. Turn to grease all sides of dough, cover with damp cloth and let rise until double. Punch down, shape rolls as desired. Cover, let rise until double. Bake at 375° for 20 minutes or until browned. Makes 4 1/2 to 5 dozen.

# POTATO FLAKE BISCUITS

1/2 cup potato flakes
1 cup flour
1 Tbs. baking powder
1/4 tsp. baking soda
1 tsp. sugar
1 tsp. salt
1/3 cup shortening
2/3 cup milk, plus 2 Tbs.

In a bowl, mix dry ingredients together, cut in shortening with pastry cutter. Add milk, stir only until moistened. Turn out on lightly floured board, pat out to 3/4 inch thick, cut into biscuits. Bake at 400° for 25 minutes. Makes 6 biscuits.

# MEXICAN POTATO CORN BREAD

3/4 cup flour
3/4 cup potato flakes
1 cup corn meal
1 Tbs. sugar
1 tsp. salt
1 Tbs. baking powder
milk
1 (15.4 oz.) can well drained corn, reserving juice
2 eggs
1/3 cup oil
4 to 5 strips of bacon, cooked crisp and crumbled
1 1/2 Tbs. grated onion
2 Tbs. finely minced green chili peppers
3/4 cup grated Cheddar cheese

In a bowl, mix first 6 ingredients. Add enough milk to reserved corn juice to make 1 1/2 cups of liquid. Add liquid, eggs and oil to flour mixture. Stir in bacon, onion, green chili peppers and corn, fold in cheese. Pour into buttered 6 x 10 baking dish. Bake at 400° for 30 minutes or until golden brown.

# DOUGHNUTS

## HINTS FOR FRYING DOUGHNUTS

As soon as the doughnuts have surfaced in the hot oil, they should be turned, this will seal the doughnut to keep it from absorbing the grease. Continue to brown on both sides.

To test the hot oil for the right temperature, place a 1-inch square cube of bread in the hot oil and when it browns in 1 minute the oil is ready.

## SPUDNUTS

1 cup shortening
1 cup sugar
3 eggs, beaten
6 Tbs. active dry yeast
1 Tbs. sugar
1 cup warm water
1 1/2 cups mashed potatoes
2 tsp. salt
3 cups warm milk
10 to 11 cups flour

In a bowl, cream shortening and sugar, add eggs. In a small bowl, mix yeast, 1 Tbs. sugar and warm water. Add to shortening mixture. Add potatoes and salt. Add milk and flour alternately. Knead 7 minutes until smooth. Let rise about 1 hour. Roll dough about 1/2 inch thick, cut into doughnuts. Deep fry in hot oil, 370° until golden brown on both sides. Drain on rack or paper towels. While still hot, roll in sugar or powdered sugar as desired. Makes 6 to 7 dozen.

# SPUD CLOUD DOUGHNUTS

1/2 cup mashed potatoes
1/4 cup sugar
1 pkg. active dry yeast
1 tsp. salt
1/4 tsp. baking powder
1/4 tsp. baking soda
3/4 cup milk
1/4 cup cooking oil
1 tsp. vanilla
1 egg, well beaten
2 1/2 to 2 3/4 cup flour
sugar and cinnamon

In a bowl, combine potatoes, sugar, yeast, salt, baking powder, baking soda, milk, oil and vanilla. Let stand in warm place for 30 minutes or until slightly bubbly. Add egg and enough flour to make a soft dough. Turn out on lightly floured surface, knead until smooth, about 5 minutes. Place in greased bowl, turning once. Cover and let rise in warm place for 45 minutes. Roll out about 1/2 inch, cut into doughnuts, carefully place on a lightly floured baking sheet. Let rise until doubled, about 30 minutes. Fry in deep hot oil, 370°, turning once, until golden brown, 45 seconds to 1 minute. Roll in sugar and cinnamon while still warm. Makes 1 1/2 to 2 dozen.

# OLD FASHIONED DROP POTATO DOUGHNUTS

1/4 cup butter
3/4 cup sugar
3 egg yolks
1 egg white
1 cup mashed potatoes
2 1/4 cups flour
3 tsp. baking powder
1/2 tsp. salt
1/4 tsp. nutmeg
1/4 cup milk

Cream butter and sugar, add egg yolks. Beat together, egg white and potatoes then add to creamed butter and sugar. Sift flour, baking powder, salt and nutmeg together. Add milk and flour alternately to creamed mixture. Spoon 1 Tbs. of dough into hot oil. Turn twice, brown evenly. Drain on rack. Cool, and roll in powdered sugar or granulated sugar.

# QUICK POTATO DOUGHNUTS

1 cup mashed potatoes
2/3 cup sugar
2 eggs, well beaten
1 cup buttermilk
2 Tbs. melted butter
4 cups sifted flour
2 tsp. baking powder
1 tsp. baking soda
2/3 tsp. salt
2 tsp. cinnamon
1/4 tsp. nutmeg

Prepare mashed potatoes, set aside. Add sugar slowly to eggs, beating continually. Stir in potato, add buttermilk and butter. Resift flour with baking powder, baking soda, salt, cinnamon and nutmeg. Stir sifted ingredients into potato mixture until well blended. Chill dough about 1 1/2 to 2 hours, until easy to handle. Fry in deep hot oil, 370°. May be cut into strips or doughnuts. Makes 2 1/2 dozen.

# POTATO CINNAMON ROLLS

1/2 cup shortening
2 cups scalded milk
2 eggs, beaten
1 tsp. salt
1/2 cup sugar
1 cup mashed potatoes
2 pkgs. active dry yeast
1/4 cup lukewarm water
7 cups sifted flour
1 cup raisins
1 cup chopped nuts
butter
cinnamon and sugar

In a large mixing bowl, dissolve shortening in hot milk, stir in eggs, salt, sugar and potatoes. In a small bowl, dissolve yeast in lukewarm water, add to potato mixture. Stir in flour, raisins and walnuts, mix thoroughly. Let rise until doubled. Roll out 1/2 inch thick on floured surface, spread with softened butter. Sprinkle with sugar and cinnamon. Carefully roll up, seal the edges. Turn edges to surface and cut into 1 1/2 inch slices. Place in well-greased baking pans 1 inch apart, let rise until light. Bake at 350° until golden brown. Then frost or cover with a glaze.

## Glaze

1 cup powdered sugar
2 Tbs. milk
1 tsp. vanilla
1 Tbs. butter
dash of salt

In a bowl, mix all ingredients together. Drizzle over cinnamon rolls or doughnuts.

# CAKES

## POTATO CHOCOLATE SPICE CAKE

4 eggs, separated
2 cups sugar
1 cup butter or margarine
3 squares melted chocolate
1 1/2 cups mashed potato
1 1/2 cups flour
2 tsp. baking powder
1 tsp. cinnamon
1/4 tsp. cloves
1/4 tsp. allspice
1/4 tsp. nutmeg
1/2 cup sweet milk
1 cup chopped walnuts

Beat egg whites to stiff peaks, set aside. Cream sugar and butter, add melted chocolate, potatoes and egg yolks. Beat 4 minutes. Combine dry ingredients, and add alternately with milk. Add walnuts, fold in egg whites. Bake 45 minutes at 350° or until done to touch. If using 9 x 13 inch pan bake 10 to 15 minutes longer.

# POTATO SPICE CAKE

4 eggs, separated
2 cups sugar
3/4 cup butter or margarine
1 tsp. vanilla
1 cup dry mashed potatoes
2 cups flour
1 tsp. soda
2 tsp. baking powder
1/2 tsp. nutmeg
1/2 tsp. allspice
1 tsp. cinnamon
·1 cup buttermilk

Beat egg whites to stiff peaks, set aside. Cream sugar and butter, add beaten egg yolks and vanilla. Add dry mashed potato, beat until light and fluffy, 4 minutes. Sift dry ingredients, add alternately with buttermilk. Fold in stiffly beaten egg whites. Pour into greased, floured 9 x 13 pan. Bake 350° for 40 to 45 minutes.

# POTATO BUTTER CREAM FROSTING

1/3 cup cold unseasoned mashed potatoes
1/3 cup margarine or butter
1 tsp. vanilla
up to 4 cups powdered sugar

### Variations

Select as many ingredients as desired
1/3 cup chopped walnuts
1/3 cup coconut
1/4 tsp. cinnamon
2 to 4 Tbs. cocoa
1 tsp. almond or other extract

Cream potatoes and margarine, add extract. Gradually add powdered sugar until proper frosting consistency.

# CHOCOLATE POTATO CAKE

4 squares unsweetened baking chocolate
1 cup hot mashed potatoes
4 eggs
1 cup butter
2 cups sugar
1 tsp. vanilla
1 tsp. almond extract
1/2 tsp. salt
3 tsp. baking powder
2 1/2 cups sifted cake flour
1/2 cup milk
1 cup finely chopped walnuts

In a double boiler pan, melt the chocolate. In a small bowl, add melted chocolate to hot mashed potatoes. Separate the yolks and whites of eggs and beat each separately. In a mixing bowl, cream butter and sugar, add the beaten yolks, vanilla, and almond. Sift the salt and baking powder with the flour. Add the potato-chocolate mixture to the creamed sugar and butter mixture. Add the flour mixture alternately with the milk. Add the chopped walnuts. Fold in the beaten egg whites. Bake in two 9-inch or three 8-inch layer pans, well greased and floured. Bake at 350° for 35 minutes, or until springs back when lightly touched in center.

# RICH CHOCOLATE FROSTING

1 stick margarine (1/2 cup)
1/4 cup cocoa
1/3 cup buttermilk
1 cup small marshmallows
1 (1 lb.) box powdered sugar (about 3 to 3/12 cups)
1 tsp. vanilla

In a sauce pan, melt first 4 ingredients together and bring to a boil. Add powdered sugar and vanilla. Mix well. May add 1/2 cup chopped walnuts and 1 cup miniature marshmallows. Frost cake.

# POTATO LOG CAKE

1/2 cup shortening
1/2 cup sugar
1/2 cup molasses
1/2 cup honey
1 egg
1 cup mashed potatoes
2 1/2 cup sifted flour
2 tsp. baking soda
1 tsp. cinnamon
1/2 tsp. ginger
1/2 tsp. salt
1/3 cup hot water
1/3 cup walnuts
1/3 cup raisins or other fruits

In a bowl, cream shortening with sugar, molasses and honey. Add egg and potatoes, blend well. Sift all dry ingredients together. Mix dry ingredients and water alternately to creamed mixture. Mix in walnuts and fruits. Pour into bread loaf pan and bake in slow oven 325° for 1 1/4 hours.

To make a Christmas Yule Log bake in 2 foil lined fruit juice cans at 325°. Place on a tray with dates or prunes on toothpicks to make knots on the log cake. Frost with a white frosting, pile on top and let frosting spill over sides on to tray. Place some holly leaves around logs.

# OATMEAL POTATO CAKE

1 1/2 cups boiling water
1 cup oatmeal
3 eggs, separated
1 cup granulated sugar
1 cup packed brown sugar
1 cup mashed potatoes, seasoned
2 tsp. vanilla
1/2 cup oil
1 3/4 cup flour
1 tsp. salt
2 tsp. baking soda
2 tsp. cinnamon

Combine oatmeal with boiling water, set aside. In a mixing bowl, cream together egg yokes, sugars, potatoes, vanilla and oil. Add flour, salt, soda and cinnamon. Add oatmeal and mix well. Beat egg whites until stiff, fold into batter. Pour into greased and floured 13 x 9 baking pan. Bake at 350° for 40 to 45 minutes or until done. May be served while warm with whipped topping or topping below.

## Topping

1 cup coconut
1 cup packed brown sugar
6 Tbs. melted butter
1/2 cup chopped walnuts
1/4 cup evaporated milk

Mix all ingredients well, spread over cake. Place under a broiler and broil until light brown and crunchy.

## POTATO OATMEAL COOKIES

1/2 cup raw grated potato
1/2 cup honey
1/4 cup melted shortening
1 egg, beaten
1 cup flour
1 cup quick cooking oatmeal
1 tsp. baking powder
1/4 tsp. soda
1/4 tsp. salt
1/2 tsp. cinnamon
1/4 tsp. nutmeg
1/2 cup raisins
1/2 cup chopped pecans

Mix first 4 ingredients together. Mix all remaining ingredients with flour and combine with first mixture. Drop by spoonfuls on greased baking sheet. Bake 350° for 15 minutes. 2 1/2 dozen cookies.

## POTATO CHIP COOKIES

1 cup butter
1 cup packed brown sugar
1 cup white sugar
2 eggs, beaten
1 tsp. vanilla
2 cups flour
1 tsp. baking soda
2 cups crushed potato chips
1 (6 oz.) pkg. chocolate chips
1/2 cup chopped walnuts

Cream butter and sugars together, add beaten eggs and vanilla. Sift flour and soda, add to creamed mixture. Add crushed potato chips, chocolate chips and walnuts. Drop by spoonfuls on lightly greased baking pan. Bake 350° for 8 to 10 minutes.

# POTATO SPICE COOKIES
## (EGG FREE)

1 cup molasses
3/4 cup shortening
1 1/2 cups potatoes, put through a sieve
1/2 tsp. salt
2 cups flour
2 tsp. baking powder
1/2 tsp. baking soda
1 tsp. cinnamon
1/4 tsp. cloves
1/2 tsp. nutmeg
1 tsp. vanilla
1/2 cup chopped walnuts
1/2 cup chopped raisins

In a bowl, combine molasses and shortening. Heat potatoes in microwave. Add molasses and shortening to potatoes, stir until shortening is melted. Add dry ingredients, sifted together. Add vanilla, walnuts and raisins, mix well. Drop by teaspoonful on a greased cookie sheet. Bake at 350° for 12 to 15 minutes. Makes 5 dozen.

# POTATO CHOCOLATE CHIP COOKIES

3/4 cup margarine
1 cup packed brown sugar
1/2 cup granulated sugar
1/2 cup cooked grated potatoes
1 tsp. vanilla
2 eggs
2 cups flour
1 tsp. baking soda
1 cup chopped walnuts
1 cup chocolate chips

In a bowl, cream margarine, sugars, potatoes, and vanilla until light and fluffy. Add eggs and beat well. Combine flour and baking soda, add to creamed mixture. Stir in walnuts and chocolate chips. Drop by teaspoonfuls on an ungreased cookie sheet. Bake at 375° for 8 to 10 minutes. Makes 5 to 6 dozen cookies. If crisp cookies are desired use potatoes which have been baked, peeled and grated while still warm. If a more cake cookie is desired use potatoes which have been boiled in their skins, peeled and grated while still warm and add 1/4 cup more flour.

# CHOCOLATE POTATO COOKIES

2(12 oz.) pkg. chocolate chips
2 (12 oz.) pkg. butterscotch chips
1 large can shoestring potatoes
1 1/2 cups chopped pecans

Melt the chips in a double boiler. Mix in potatoes and pecans. Drop by spoonfuls onto lightly buttered baking pan. Chill until set. Makes 4 dozen.

# DOUBLE CHOCOLATE POTATO DROPS

1/4 cup shortening or margarine
1 cup packed brown sugar
1/2 cup cold mashed potatoes
1 egg, beaten
3 squares melted unsweetened chocolate
1 tsp. vanilla
1 1/2 cups sifted flour
1/8 tsp. salt
1/2 tsp. baking soda
3/4 cup buttermilk
1/2 cup toasted pecans
chocolate icing

In a bowl, cream together shortening and sugar, beat in potatoes, egg, chocolate, and vanilla until well blended. Sift together flour, salt and soda. Add flour mixture alternately with buttermilk to the batter. Stir in pecans. Drop by teaspoonfuls on greased cookie sheet. Bake 375° for 10 minutes. Frost if desired while cookies are warm. Makes 4 to 5 dozen cookies.

# FUDGE ICING

1 stick butter
2 squares melted unsweetened chocolate
6 Tbs. milk
1 (1 lb.) box powdered sugar
1 tsp. vanilla

In a sauce pan, combine butter, unsweetened chocolate and milk. Heat and stir until very smooth. Beat in powdered sugar and vanilla. Beat until smooth. Spread on top of cookies.

# CANDY

## POTATO FONDANT

1/2 cup unseasoned mashed potatoes, (not instant potatoes)
3 cups sifted powdered sugar
1 cup moist coconut, flaked or shredded
1 tsp. vanilla

Combine mashed potatoes, sugar, coconut, and vanilla in mixing bowl. Cream with wooden spoon or electric mixer as for making cake. Chill mixture in refrigerator for several hours. Remove and turn on to damp surface of baking sheet. Knead with hands until mixture is creamy. Shape into 1 inch balls. Will store in air tight container for about 2 weeks. About 1 1/2 lbs. or 60 one inch balls.

### Variations

### Christmas Mints

Omit vanilla and substitute a few drops of oil of peppermint. Tint fondant pink with food coloring. Flatten balls to about 1/4 inch thickness.

### Candied Fruit Balls

Omit vanilla and substitute rum, lemon, or maple flavoring. Add 1 cup finely chopped candied cherries, pineapple, apricots, or dates. Dried orange or lemon peel may be used. Allow confections to dry at room temperature for at least 24 hours. These keep well at room temperature if covered with plastic wrap.

### Coffee Mocha Logs

Add 2 tsp. instant powdered coffee to recipe while kneading mixture. Shape into rolls 1/2 x 2 inches, roll in chocolate sprinkles.

### Coated Potato Balls

Roll balls in coconut or finely chopped walnuts.

# BLACK AND WHITE POTATO SQUARES

1/2 cup mashed potatoes
2 tsp. melted margarine or butter
1 tsp. vanilla
4 cups powdered sugar
1 1/2 cups coconut (or more if desired)
3 oz. semi-sweet chocolate (either 1/2 cup chips or 3 squares)
crushed walnuts

In a bowl, combine potato, melted margarine and vanilla. Add powdered sugar gradually, then coconut, blend well. Press into greased and waxed paper lined 8 x 8 pan. The candy will be 1/2 inch thick, cool. Melt chocolate and pour evenly over top, working quickly to spread. If desired sprinkle crushed walnuts and pat into chocolate. Chill until firm, cut into small pieces. Stores well if kept covered in refrigerator.

## Variations

### Hay Stacks

Form white mixture into cones 1 inch high. Allow to stand uncovered, for 20 minutes. Dip the base of each cone in melted chocolate, place on wax paper until chocolate hardens.

### Chocolate Rolls

Roll candy into 1 1/2 inches in diameter. Spread melted chocolate on roll. Chill 2 hours, cut into 1/4 to 1/2 inch slices to serve.

# QUICK POTATO FUDGE

2 squares bitter chocolate or 6 Tbs. cocoa and 1 Tbs. butter
3 Tbs. butter
1/3 cup mashed potatoes
1/8 tsp. salt
1 tsp. vanilla
4 cups sifted powdered sugar

In a double boiler, melt the chocolate and butter together. Add the mashed potatoes, salt and vanilla. Blend in the sugar. Knead until smooth. Shape into a long roll, 1 inch in diameter, cool and cut into slices. Or candy may be pressed into buttered waxed paper lined 8 inch square pan, cooled and cut into squares. Makes 1 1/4 lbs.

# POTATO COCONUT FUDGE

4 Tbs. melted butter
1 cup shredded coconut
2 tsp. vanilla
2 cups powdered sugar
2 medium potatoes, cooked and mashed
4 squares melted sweet chocolate

In a bowl, add butter, coconut, vanilla and powdered sugar to the mashed potatoes, beat until creamy. Pour into 8 x 11 buttered pan. When set, top with melted chocolate. Let cool and cut into squares.

# SOURDOUGH RECIPES

## MASHED POTATO SOURDOUGH STARTER

3 medium potatoes, peeled and diced
4 cups boiling water
1 pkg. active dry yeast
1 cup lukewarm water
1 cup sifted flour
1/3 cup sugar
1 1/2 tsp. salt

In a sauce pan, cook potatoes in boiling water until tender, drain, saving liquid. Mash potatoes and return to liquid. Cool to lukewarm. Dissolve yeast in 1 cup lukewarm water and add to mashed potatoes. Stir in remaining ingredients, pour into a clean glass or plastic container. Cover with towel and let set in warm place for 2 or 3 days or until mixture ferments. Use at this time or store in refrigerator in a clean container. Cover of container should have a small hole punched to allow gases to escape. Replenish with equal portions of warm water and flour added to starter. Allow to ferment at room temperature for 8 to 10 hours. Cover and return to refrigerator. If starter is not used and replenished once a week, stir down after 3 or 4 weeks, discard half of it and replenish the balance with same recipe first used. A sprinkle of dry yeast may be needed if starter doesn't appear bubbly and fermented after being in use for a period of time. If a clear liquid forms on top of mixture, stir down and continue to use as needed.

# MOM'S SOURDOUGH BREAD

2 heaping Tbs. wheat germ
2 Tbs. soy flour
rye flour
1 cup whole wheat flour
1/3 cup sugar
1 tsp. salt
1/2 cup oil
2 cups potato sourdough starter
2 pkgs. active dry yeast, dissolved in 1/4 cup warm water
1 cup water
5 1/2 to 6 1/2 cups unbleached flour

    In a cup, place wheat germ and soy flour, finish filling the cup with rye flour. In a large mixing bowl, add rye mixture with the whole wheat flour. Add sugar and salt. Mix the oil, starter, yeast and water together, add to whole wheat flour mixture, mixing well. Add enough unbleached flour so that dough is easy to knead. Knead dough until elastic, 8 to 10 minutes. Place in a greased bowl, turning dough to grease top, cover with a cloth and let rise in a warm place free from draft until doubled. Make into 2 loaves, let rise until doubled. Bake at 350° for 35 to 40 minutes.

# SOURDOUGH BREAD

1 cup potato sourdough starter
2 cups lukewarm water
2 cups flour
1 cup milk
3 Tbs. butter
3 Tbs. sugar
2 tsp. salt
2 pkgs. active dry yeast, dissolved in 1/4 cup warm water
7 cups flour
1 tsp. baking soda

In a large mixing bowl, add starter, water and 2 cups flour, mix well. Let stand, covered, in a warm place over night. Next day heat milk and stir in butter, 2 Tbs. sugar and 1 tsp. salt, cool to lukewarm. Add yeast into cooled milk mixture, add to starter mixture. Beat until mixed well. Beat in 2 cups of flour until batter is smooth. Mix baking soda with remaining sugar and salt, sift evenly over dough and stir gently to mix well. Cover with cloth, set in a warm place and let rise 40 minutes or until doubled in size. Mix dough and gradually beat in rest of flour until dough forms a ball. Turn out onto floured surface and knead until smooth and elastic, about 5 minutes, adding more flour if necessary. Divide dough in half, cover and let rest for 10 minutes. Shape into loaves and place into greased loaf pans. Brush tops with oil, let rise about 1 hour, or until loaves are light. Bake at 375° for 40 minutes.

# POTATO SOURDOUGH BREAD WITH BACON

2 pkgs. active dry yeast
1/2 cup lukewarm water
1 1/2 cups water
2 cups sharp shredded Cheddar cheese
3/4 cup bacon, cooked crisp and crumbled
1 tsp. baking powder
2 Tbs. sugar
2 Tbs. salt
3 Tbs. melted butter
2 cups mashed potatoes
1 1/2 cups potato sourdough starter
7 to 7 1/2 cups flour

In a small bowl dissolve yeast in lukewarm water. In a large bowl mix together water, cheese, bacon, baking powder, sugar, salt, butter and potatoes to starter. Stir in yeast and mix well. Mix in 1 cup flour at a time, blending well after each addition. Turn out on floured surface, knead until smooth and elastic, adding more flour if necessary. Place dough in a greased bowl turning once to grease surface, cover with a cloth. Place in a warm place free from draft and let rise until doubled. Divide dough in half and shape into loaves, place into loaf pans, cover. Let rise in warm place for about 2 hours until doubled. Bake at 375° for 40 to 45 minutes. Makes 2 loaves.

# SOURDOUGH WHOLE WHEAT OATMEAL BREAD

2 pkgs. active dry yeast
1/2 cup lukewarm water
1 1/2 cups boiling water
1 1/2 cups quick cooking oatmeal
2/3 cup molasses
1/3 cup oil
1 Tbs. salt
6 cups whole wheat flour
1 1/4 cups potato sourdough starter
2 eggs, beaten

In a small bowl dissolve yeast in lukewarm water. In a large mixing bowl, combine boiling water, oats, molasses, oil and salt, cool to lukewarm. Stir in 2 1/2 cups flour and mix well. Add starter, yeast and eggs. Stir in enough flour to make a soft dough, turn out on a lightly floured surface, knead 8 minutes, until smooth and elastic. Place in a lightly greased bowl turning to grease surface, cover. Place in a warm place, let rise about 2 hours until doubled in size. Punch down, turn onto lightly floured surface. Divide dough in half, cover and let rest 10 minutes. Form into 2 loaves and place into well greased loaf pans. Cover and let rise in a warm place until doubled. Bake at 375° for 45 minutes. Makes 2 loaves.

# FLUFFY SOURDOUGH BISCUITS

1 cup potato sourdough starter
1 tsp. sugar
2 tsp. active dry yeast
2 Tbs. lukewarm water
1 1/2 tsp. baking powder
3/4 tsp. salt
1 1/2 cups flour
4 Tbs. shortening
1/4 cup melted butter

In a bowl, mix starter and sugar. Dissolve yeast in lukewarm water, add to potato sourdough starter. In a bowl combine baking powder, salt and flour, cut in shortening until it resembles coarse cornmeal. Add to starter, stirring well. Turn out onto lightly floured surface, knead 6 to 8 times adding more flour if necessary. Roll dough out to 1/2 inch thickness, cut into biscuits and place in baking pan. Brush tops of biscuits with melted butter. Cover with a cloth, set in warm place and let rise for 1 hour. Bake at 400° for 20 minutes or until golden brown. Makes 12 biscuits.

# SOURDOUGH PANCAKES

2 cups flour
1 3/4 cups lukewarm water
3/4 cup potato sourdough starter
2 Tbs. sugar
1 tsp. salt
1 tsp. baking powder
1/4 cup melted butter
2 eggs
3/4 tsp. baking soda, dissolved in 1 Tbs. water

In a bowl, combine flour, water and starter, beat until smooth and let stand in warm place over night. Add to the batter sugar, salt, baking powder, butter and eggs, beating well. Fold in baking soda and water mixture. Do not stir after the baking soda has been added. Cook pancakes on a hot lightly oiled skillet

# SOURDOUGH APPLE OATMEAL MUFFINS

1 cup potato sourdough starter
1/2 cup milk
1 egg
1/4 cup melted butter
1/2 cup honey
1 1/4 cup applesauce
1/2 tsp. salt
1 1/2 tsp. baking powder
1 1/2 cups whole wheat flour
1 1/4 cups quick cooking oatmeal

In a mixing bowl, combine starter, milk, egg, butter, honey and applesauce, mix well. In a bowl mix together salt, baking powder, flour and oats. Add to the starter mixture and stir just until moistened. Fill greased muffin tin cups 2/3rds full. Bake at 400° for 18 to 20 minutes or until done. Makes 14 muffins.

# SOURDOUGH BRAN MUFFINS

1/2 cup potato sourdough starter
1 egg
1/2 cup honey
1/4 cup melted butter
2/3 cup milk
1/2 tsp. salt
1 tsp. baking soda
1 cup whole wheat flour
2/3 cup whole bran cereal
1/2 cup raisins

In a mixing bowl, combine starter, egg, honey, butter and milk, mix well. In a bowl mix together salt, soda and flour, add to sourdough mixture, stirring just until moistened. Fold in bran and raisins. Fill greased muffin pan cups 3/4 full. Bake at 400° for 20 minutes or until done. Makes 12 muffins.

# SOURDOUGH PIZZA CRUST

1 1/2 cups potato sourdough starter
1 cup warm water
1 1/2 tsp. salt
1 Tbs. sugar
2 tsp. active dry yeast
2 Tbs. melted shortening
3 to 3 1/2 cups flour

In a mixing bowl, combine starter, water, salt, sugar, yeast and shortening. Add flour, a small amount at a time, blending well after each addition. Add enough flour to make dough stiff but elastic. Turn out onto floured surface, knead 7 minutes. Place dough in a greased bowl, turning to grease surface. Cover with a cloth, set in a warm place and let rise until doubled. Divide dough in half, stretch dough out to fit 2 (10 to 12 inch) round pizza pans. Brush with oil before adding toppings. Top with favorite toppings. Bake at 425° for about 25 minutes. Makes 2 pizza crusts.

# SOURDOUGH CREPES

3 eggs, beaten
1 3/4 cups potato sourdough starter
1 cup milk
2 Tbs. sugar
1/4 tsp. salt
1/3 tsp. baking soda
2 Tbs. melted butter
1/2 cup flour

In a mixing bowl, beat together eggs, starter and milk, add sugar, salt, baking soda, butter and flour, blending well. Heat a 6 inch skillet to medium hot, sprayed with non-stick spray. Pour in enough batter to cover bottom, tip skillet back and forth to spread batter evenly to make a thin crepe. Cook each side until light brown. Crepes may be cooked in advance and refrigerated. Heat before serving. Crepes may be filled and rolled with favorite filling.

# SOURDOUGH POTATO DOUGHNUTS

2 pkg. active dry yeast
1/2 cup warm water
2 cups scalded milk
1/2 cup shortening
1/2 cup sugar
2 tsp. salt
1 1/2 cups cooked mashed potatoes
2 eggs, beaten
1 cup potato sourdough starter
7 to 7 1/2 cups flour

In a small bowl dissolve yeast in warm water, set aside. Add to scalded milk in saucepan, shortening, sugar and salt, cool. In a larger mixing bowl, combine mashed potatoes, eggs and starter. Add milk mixture and yeast, mixing well. Add flour slowly until dough pulls away from side of the mixing bowl. Turn out onto floured surface and knead for 3 minutes. Let rest for 5 minutes. Roll dough to 1/2 inch thick, cut with doughnut cutter and place on lightly floured baking sheet, cover with a cloth and set in a warm place. Let rise for about 40 to 45 minutes. Fry in hot oil at until golden brown. Roll in sugar or powdered sugar or may be glazed or frosted. Makes 3 1/2 dozen.

# SOURDOUGH POTATO BROWNIES

4 ozs. unsweetened chocolate squares
2/3 cup shortening
1 1/4 cups mashed potatoes, no milk or seasoning
1 3/4 cups sugar
4 eggs
1 cup potato sourdough starter
1 cup flour
1 tsp. salt
1 tsp. baking powder
1 cup chopped walnuts
2 tsp. vanilla

In a sauce pan, melt chocolate and shortening over low heat, stirring constantly. In a mixing bowl, combine potatoes, chocolate mixture, sugar, eggs and starter. Stir together flour, salt, baking powder and walnuts, add to chocolate mixture. Add vanilla, mixing well. Pour into a 9 x 13 baking dish. Bake at 350° for 30 minutes or until done. Frost if desired.

# SOURDOUGH APPLESAUCE COOKIES

1 cup shortening
2 cups sugar
2 eggs
1 cup potato sourdough starter
5 cups flour
1 1/2 tsp. baking soda
2 tsp. cinnamon
2 cups unsweetened applesauce
2 cups raisins
1 1/2 cups chopped walnuts

In a bowl, cream shortening with sugar, add eggs and beat until fluffy. Add starter. Mix together dry ingredients and add alternately with applesauce to batter. Add raisins and walnuts. Drop by teaspoonful onto greased baking sheets. Bake at 350° for 15 minutes or until done. Makes 5 to 6 dozen.

# SOURDOUGH APPLESAUCE CAKE

1 1/2 cups sugar
1/2 cup shortening
2 eggs
1 cup potato sourdough starter
1 3/4 cups applesauce
2 cups flour
1 1/2 tsp. cinnamon
1/2 tsp. ground allspice
1 1/2 tsp. salt
1 tsp. baking soda
1 tsp. baking powder
1 tsp. vanilla
1 tsp. almond flavoring
1 cup raisins
1 cup chopped walnuts

In a mixing bowl, cream sugar and shortening together, add eggs and mix well. Add starter and applesauce. With a mixer beat on high speed for 2 minutes. Sift flour, spices, salt, baking soda and baking powder together. Add alternately with flavorings to batter. Beat each addition until smooth. Stir in raisins and walnuts. Pour batter into greased and floured tube pan. Bake at 350° for 1 hour and 15 minutes or until done. Cool in pan for 10 minutes then turn out onto rack to finish cooling. Slice and serve with whipped cream.

# SOURDOUGH CARROT CAKE

2 cups flour
2 tsp. baking powder
2 tsp. salt
1 tsp. baking soda
2 tsp. cinnamon
1 tsp. allspice
8 eggs, separated
1 cup packed brown sugar
1/2 cup granulated sugar
1 cup oil
1 cup potato sourdough starter
2 cups raw grated carrots
1 cup raisins

In a mixing bowl, combine flour, baking powder, salt, baking soda and spices, set aside. In a bowl, beat egg whites until peaks form, set aside. In a large bowl, combine sugars, oil, egg yolks and starter, mix in carrots and raisins. Blend in dry ingredients. Fold egg whites into batter. Pour batter into 2 well greased tube pans. Bake at 350° for 30 minutes or until done. Cool in pans for 10 minutes then turn out onto rack to finish cooling. Makes 2 cakes.

# Index

# MAIN DISHES, SIDE DISHES AND CASSEROLES

## GRAVIES AND SAUCES

# BAKED POTATOES AND TOPPINGS

# SOUPS

## SALADS

# LO-CAL AND LOW SODIUM

# BREAKFAST

# APPETIZERS

# SWEET POTATOES

# BREADS

# DOUGHNUTS

# CAKES

# COOKIES

# CANDY

# SOURDOUGH RECIPES